CU00597136

How to be great at Customer Service
The essence of great customer service

By

Mario Dolcezza

Published
by

Rotherfield Studio Ltd

How to be Great at Customer Service
The Essence of Great Customer Service

by

Mario Dolcezza

Copyright Infomation

ISBN 978-0-9566304-2-1
First Published September 2011
Rotherfield Studio Ltd

Cover Photograph
By
Nick Tolley

Text set in Bembo by Rotherfield Studio Ltd
E-mail sales@rotherfieldstudio.com

Registered office 14 Wellington Square Hastings East Sussex TN34 1PB

Printed in England by Berforts Group Ltd

Contents

So why is customer service important?

It really pains me how dumb some businesses can be. They take their customers for granted, invest little in their relationships and expect the money to come rolling in by just opening the doors.

The credit crunch can be said to have had at least one positive effect in so much that it has made many such blasé companies think twice about their customer service, which despite being forced upon them by recession and competition they still do almost reluctantly.

I really don't understand why customers are not treated as if they were the single most important thing to every business. I mean isn't it obvious? Customers are the one thing that without every business is guaranteed to fail.

Without customers we cannot grow our businesses. We invest huge sums in attracting more and more new customers but only a fraction of this on caring for the ones we already have.

We teach our staff how to follow the processes we have set in place and to do their job well, they learn how to stack shelves, formulate proposals, serve food, arrange finance. In fact we invest heavily in giving our staff all the skills they need to do their jobs and yet we barely give them any practical know-how at all on how to look after our customers well.

And when we get it wrong and fail to deliver on even the basic levels of good customer service we look to minimise our costs for putting things right, without a thought for the impact of a negative experience on our businesses reputation or concern for an unhappy customer.

The fact is that if you were completely ruthless, self-centred and unflinchingly commercial it would make no difference as great customer service makes complete financial sense.

Happy, delighted customers have certain qualities that are essential to a profitable business. For starters they're much less sensitive to price, don't get me wrong price is always an important factor, but for these customers it's not the most important factor. Other considerations such as their relationship with you, how they feel when they deal with your company and the experience they have

1

are all key.

Happy, delighted customers feel valued and important and are often known on first name terms, they are more receptive to being sold ancillary products and services and are your greatest sales people often feeling compelled to introduce new customers to your business.

Happy, delighted customers are far more forgiving of our minor failings and indiscretions, making excuses for us rather than making complaints, they are the easiest to please and slowest to criticise.

So when you consider all of these things it seems obvious that if you gave every single customer that visited your premises an insurmountable buying experience, life would be so incredibly easy!

Our marketing budget could be slashed, after all most of our customers come to us not because of our media messages but because of glowing recommendations. We wouldn't have to cut our prices to compete because our customers don't buy on price alone, they buy from us because they know that they're going to get a fabulous buying experience. Moreover our customers don't worry themselves about the relationship after the sale, they know that we're always going to look after them and this guarantees their custom for many, many years, if not forever!

Our focus on customer service means that we're a highly profitable organisation, which in turn means that we can give our customers a service that is second to none. This guarantees our business more and more customers and as our business grows so does our reputation until one day we are the market leaders in our sector. This of course attracts more and more customers to our business, which in turn makes us more profitable and so it continues, going from strength-to-strength.

So for me, there simply is no other way to be when it comes to customers and customer service. Anything other than giving your customer a fabulous buying experience is commercially unsound; it's just not good business.

Service professionals – a raw deal?

It amazes me how so many service businesses give such little credit to the people that really matter within their organisation – the waiters, bar people, receptionists, shop assistants, in fact any customer facing staff. All of which are likely to be underpaid, poorly trained or generally taken for granted. Here's what Howard Schultz (Starbucks Coffee Chairman) says about the subject:

"It's ironic that retailers and restaurants live or die on customer service, yet their employees have some of the lowest pay and worst benefits of any industry. That's one reason so many retail experiences are mediocre for the public."

Yet it is these very people on which our service industry relies upon to ensure that our customers have an enjoyable experience and are left wanting more. So why is it that service staff are generally treated as low paid, unskilled workers? And why don't businesses invest more in training, giving service staff better customer management skills?

In today's competitive markets service is often the casualty, in fact a whole new 'no frills' industry has grown out of the trade off between service and cost. Here businesses actively reduce the customer service offered in order to reduce the overall cost to the consumer. I believe that in general most businesses have this attitude to some degree or another and see the way to greater profits through tightly managed staffing costs at the expense of customer service. So one could argue the pay reflects the level of importance they place on this role.

There are counter arguments to this position and many service focused establishments have a much more considered recruitment policy taking only the best, most vibrant staff who they pay well but demand much more from in return. These people are professional hosts, they work hard on creating a great customer experience and are well rewarded for their efforts. But great service shouldn't be just the domain of only the best establishments, it should be a part of every company's approach to business, particularly in these difficult and extremely competitive days.

So whether you are one of the undervalued, maybe you own your own establishment, or you work for a large organisation, I'm going to share with you some of the simple things that really will make a difference without making your life any harder.

The Role of The Professional Host

OK first things first – I have coined the phrase 'The Professional Host' because I believe that it's about time we considered people that work on the front-line of customer services as professionals. We should provide them with the skills and the remuneration that reflects their status as professionals. So, it's a catchall term to describe anybody that interacts directly with the customer: shop assistants, receptionists, check-in staff, waiters, sales staff, representatives etc.

Now you might not think that these people could be considered as hosts but by definition I believe that they are. My son's school dictionary defines the word as: "host – a person who has guests and looks after them". Fundamentally this is about mindset, customers will visit your shop, restaurant or whatever your business. They are there as your guests – the function of a Professional Host is to look after them. Describing customer-facing staff as hosts reminds them of the responsibility they have from the very moment the customer arrives until the time that they leave. It suggests that all aspects of that customer's visit are their responsibility and that their sole function is to ensure that the customer has a good experience.

Now for me this mindset is golden and it makes no difference whether you're selling a newspaper in a corner shop or serving at some swanky restaurant. Ensuring that the experience the customer has (no matter how short) is a positive one is essential to the future growth and prosperity of the business and, by default, the earning potential of the individual serving.

Some time ago, I happened to meet up with a slightly eccentric cheery fellow that I had met on a number of previous occasions who also worked within the customer service industry as an advisor and consultant. We got to talking about a contract he had been engaged on with a rather large French car manufacturer who wanted him to advise them on a customer service process for a top of the range premium vehicle that they wanted to sell to the upper market.

In fact what they were asking for was a better sales/customer service process for their premium car buyers than was available to the rest of their 'general' customers. We were both flabbergasted, not only was this company considering different tiers of service dependent of the type of car you were purchasing, but they were also reserving their very best level of service for their premium brand. A brand that represented only a small fraction of the cars they actually sold. It was almost upside down, establishing a quality service at the point of least volume. But what was astonishing above all else was that this business was quite prepared to be selective as to when and to whom they would offer great customer service.

With the right mindset there is only one level of customer service, any less than doing the job properly is doing the job badly. So you should never have different tiers of customer service within the same organisation. Those businesses that attempt this, risk alienating many of their customers and confusing their staff.

So at the risk of repeating myself let's make it absolutely clear, it doesn't matter what industry or service sector you're in, good service is the most important function you carry out and it should always be offered at every occasion in so far as the customer visit allows. To achieve this there are a number of 'rules' you can adopt that will help you ensure that the customer has a good experience when visiting your business.

Managing your business basics

Giving great service is not just about the way you serve the customer. It's also about a whole host of subtle things that combine to create the greater customer experience. Little things like untidy counters, dusty or empty shelves, broken light bulbs in shops or lipstick on glasses, smeared tables and empty salt cruets in pubs - all barely noticeable on their own but brought together can make a great experience really a rather mediocre one.

Many years ago I worked in the hospitality industry, which is where I developed my passion for all things customer service related. In particular I will often recount a story about a town centre pub called the Imperial or 'The Imp' in Weston-super-Mare, which I was invited to run by one of my now closest friends.

When he and I first got involved in The Imp we took on a business with a weekly turnover of around £3k yet within a year we had more than quadrupled the income, regularly exceeding £12k a week and at its utmost heights achieving an outstanding £17k per week – and this was some 20 years ago! The fact is we changed what was a very beautiful but very quiet pub into the busiest place in town!

The point is that I am often asked what was the thing we did that so radically changed the business and made it so phenomenally successful? My answer is always the same – there was no one single thing. In fact there weren't even a few things – the success of our venture was a result of an amalgamation of hundreds of little things each contributing, sometimes perhaps subconsciously to the overall experience of our guests. In fact if you asked our customers why they enjoyed visiting us so much they couldn't tell you – they just did!

But I know why our customers enjoyed the experience so much - I can pin point all of the many, many things we did to create the perfect atmosphere and I can tell you that none of it was by accident. We were successful because we looked at everything and ensured that every detail was right, all of the time. Since we left The Imp all those years ago, the business was never the same – a succession of owners never quite realised the potential of the place and were unable to replicate those perfect conditions, still time will tell. The Imp has new owners now and I sincerely hope that they are able to recreate the fantastic success we enjoyed two decades ago.

It's that attention to detail that gets missed so often at grassroots level. Is it really going to take that much more effort to leave a dining table cleaned and polished rather than the normal quick wipe over with a greasy dishcloth? And what does it take to change the odd broken light bulb? The answer of course nothing, so why do these things get missed? Well it's a combination of things, firstly small changes that happen progressively over time are difficult to notice as a whole and so we miss the fact that our business is looking tired or battered in much the same way as we miss the gradual changes to our own appearance as we grow older. The other factor I'm afraid is often down to poor housekeeping because the management team are simply too lazy, negligent or can't be bothered. Once you have ignored something that is in clear need of attention you will never see it again because it has become acceptable to you.

The way to approach this problem is through good process and a critical eye. Now, I'm not going to go through what sort of processes you should put in place because many of you will already have these and they will differ from business to business. Suffice to say that you should have a simple checklist of things that need doing every day. In pubs and restaurants this will include stocking and facing up the shelves, filling the condiments, checking the cutlery etc. In other businesses it will be different but what's key is to look at it as if you were a customer entering your premises. Take yourself step-by-step through the customer experience and examine every aspect of your visit, making a list as you go of things that would affect your experience. Remember you can add to or change the list at any time.

Over and above this, you need a monthly maintenance check to review your business appearance as a whole. Often a lick of paint can hide the scuff marks on the walls and a bit of elbow grease can tidy up scruffy or dusty out of the way areas that get missed through general cleaning – the point is if you don't keep an eye on your premises it won't take long before it's looking shabby and that will have an effect on your customers' experience.

This is a good start and will help to keep your customers in once they're through the door. However, the outer appearance of your business is perhaps even more critical as it is the only opportunity you will get to make a good first impression. I am sure that if you're anything like me you will have already been put off dealing with a company or even entering their premises because of their outward appearance.

It quite often amazes me how poor businesses are at making customers feel welcome. Our nature as human beings means that we often feel cautious and intrusive when exploring new areas that are unknown to us. Visiting somewhere that is unfamiliar to us creates a sense of unease (even if on a very low subconscious level) and it's our job to put people at ease as soon as we possibly can.

I will try and help you get a sense of what I am saying – have you ever entered a business and felt unsure that you were in the right place. Perhaps you went through a door that you thought was the right one but weren't so sure once you were through it. Perhaps you had decided to visit a business but there were gates on the entrance and they were closed – was it the right place? Should you go through the gates? Or you arrive at a destination and it all looks closed – the doors are shut and it's not clear whether they're trading or not – do you try the doors? They're open but when you're inside there's no-one about and you're still unsure if they're open.

This sort of thing goes on all the time with all sorts of businesses because they miss the first fundamental – welcoming your guests. When we as individuals have a dinner party or invite guests to our house we take great care to ensure the place is as welcoming as we can. Quite often I see houses with balloons tied to the gate to act as a marker – everyone knows that this is the right spot and they're expecting us.

We'll put the outside lights on, open the gates and if we have a porch we will leave the outer door open inviting our guests in. And, of course, when they arrive we will be there ready and waiting to greet them warmly and immediately set about making them as comfortable as we can. Yet why don't we treat our business guests, our customers in the same way?

If you ever have to entertain customers at your premises, then there a few things that you absolutely must do to welcome them and make them feel welcome:

Clearly signpost your business

Make it easy for your customers, don't leave them guessing or uncertain. Using clear signs appropriately will put your customers at ease and will even actually generate additional footfall – here are some examples:

- We are open!
- This way for a great offer
- Please come in
- Welcome
- Please ask us – we're happy to help.

And so on...

It's equally important that you manage your customers' expectations too, especially around opening times or specific trading/service requirements and try to do this with a positive spin, for example:

- Closed for now – but back again at 4.30pm!
- Please help us to help you – make sure you have all the documents needed
- Sorry – we know there's a problem but the good news is it will be fixed by Monday.

This last one is particularly important because it acknowledges an issue and shows that you are on top of the situation. If you don't do that you run the risk of your customers wondering whether you know or even care about the problem. I can illustrate this in a bit more detail for you.

One of my clients is a big hospitality business called Sanguine that operates across the UK with some quite high profile brands including the celebrated Marco Pierre White Grill and in particular 'theclub' – a small chain of award-winning health clubs and spas that are fresh and exciting.

Not far from where I live Sanguine operates the Cadbury House Hotel and leisure complex, which includes 'theclub and spa Bristol'. The guys there are very customer focused. While they don't profess to get it right all of the time they are incredibly active at engaging their customers through feedback using the system we developed and then reacting to the responses they get.

Now the team at theclub and spa Bristol are very organised and run quite a tight ship – they have clear cleaning and maintenance regimes, which are essential for the line of work that they are in. Like any good management team they identified very early that their lockers were looking a little tired and in some state of disrepair. And like any good management team they ordered a complete new set to replace the ones they had.

However, they hadn't considered the fact that if they had noticed a deterioration in their locker facilities then it would seem obvious that so would their customers too! And while the management team knew that all was in hand (having placed an order for replacement lockers), their customers would have no inkling of this. All this came to light through the fabulous feedback system we introduced to them where their members and customers were very vocal about their concerns. The problem wasn't so much that the customers were not happy about the lockers (after all they were about to get some new ones), it was more about the fact that the problem didn't appear to have been acknowledged or was addressed.

It hadn't occurred to the team at theclub and spa Bristol that they ought to let their customers know about the replacement lockers, or that by being a little more proactive and sharing information with them would make them feel more comfortable in their environment. But in any case the problem was very easily resolved with the addition of a small notice in the changing rooms: "Thanks for bearing with us – great news, new lockers in two weeks time!"

This simple statement shows that the business is on top if its game – it not only acknowledges a problem that its customers would have noticed too, but it also shows that the issue has been addressed and will be resolved. So you can see that the use of simple notices and signposts are essential to managing your customers' expectations and ensuring that their experience with you is a good one. It's all about communication and if we just assume that our customers will be familiar with what we do and how we do it, we are not going to truly generate the business we deserve.

Being available and accessible

This is kind of critical and cuts across a lot of different areas in this book.

Accessibility is how easily customers are able to contact you, whether that's in person, via the internet or over the telephone. Most customers have certain expectations in terms of what they expect when contacting a company or supplier and how this expectation is managed forms a big chunk of their opinions of us.

For example, if you run a small shop or business your customers will have certain expectations of your opening hours. They won't expect you to be shut at lunchtime if you're a café or coffee shop and they will expect you to be open on a Saturday if you're a retail outlet. These are basic expectations set by your industry and your competitors, and if you don't meet them your competitors will.

Set your opening times and stick to them. Your customers need to know when they can expect to find you available and if you constantly change this you will quickly find that they will look elsewhere.

The same can be said for how you handle telephone calls into your business. Over the years many businesses have sought to automate the way they handle calls into their business to increase efficiencies and reduce costs. Now reducing costs is ultimately good for the customer as it increases competition and drives down prices but at what expense?

I don't know of anyone that wouldn't prefer to speak with an actual real person rather than deal with the automated responder. My own experience of them can be intensely frustrating especially if the nature of your call is anything out of the ordinary.

Let me tell you in particular about Virgin, which had supplied me with broadband services for what must have been approaching 20 years. It was necessary for me to call its technical department one afternoon. Almost inevitably once I had passed the mandatory "press one for…, press two for…" I finally reached the next mandatory stage: "your call is in a queue and should be answered by the next available operator within 20 minutes". So I steeled myself for the wait.

To my great surprise a totally unexpected message cut in, something along the lines of…

"To ease the pain of waiting, why not choose which sort of music you would like to listen to, press one for dance, press two for classical…" and so on.

How good is that?

I was really impressed that someone had taken the time to think about how they might lessen the impact of waiting on the telephone. So I selected my preference and sat back to listen to the music.

Having listened to the music for some time I worked out that there were in fact only four tracks on my chosen music selection and by now they were getting rather tiresome, so much so that I almost welcomed the occasional "your call is important to us..." interjection every now and then.

By now my 20 minutes was well over half an hour and I am stewing in the inane repetitive music track, which is only serving to drive me up the wall. I had had enough and hung up!

I called back again later, I had no choice, and the whole process repeated itself again – I chose a different selection of music this time, I don't think I could have endured those four same tracks ever again! This time it didn't take as long and I got to speak with someone within five or six minutes.

Now there's a whole other story here about the lack of interest on the part of the person taking my call. The upshot for which was that my issues went unresolved and a week or two later I decided to change supplier after nearly 20 years of service. Make no mistake though, my awful experience with the Virgin automated call handling system was a key driver for this change.

Incidentally – I needed to call Virgin again to switch my broadband supplier and it will come as no surprise to many of you that when I selected the "if you're thinking of leaving us" option that I was connected to an operator within moments. I'm afraid that it was all rather too little too late and despite the best efforts of the operator to cut his charges, even though this was refused on a previous occasion, I had made up my mind to leave and doubt that I will ever return.

Virgin was simply not accessible, I accepted that I would have to endure a degree of faffing around and waiting but it was just too long. It gave me no real sense that I was important to Virgin – I wouldn't keep my customers waiting on the telephone for more than half an hour! If you run automated telephone handling systems don't push your customers' patience and ensure that you get a real person on the telephone as soon as you can. And if that's likely to be a while get more staff in!

Most big businesses are like this. It seems that the bigger you become the less likely you are to have that personal touch. British Gas does a clever job of putting some reverse spin on it – its television advert promised to answer your call within 60 seconds or its team would call you back within the hour. Sounds good in principle but when I'm calling British Gas I do so at my convenience and if they don't answer I am inconvenienced. When British Gas call me it does so at its convenience, not mine and if I'm busy I'm inconvenienced again. I think that all businesses, especially the big ones, need to think again about how they handle calls.

Perhaps the biggest hot potato for customer call handling systems is the seemingly insatiable desire for companies to outsource their call handling to overseas call centres.

Quite frankly there has been so much negative, bad press on businesses employing this practice that I'm astounded that there are companies out there that still do this. The fact of the matter is that customers don't like overseas call centres and this is principally due to poor communicative skills, where call centre operatives simply cannot be understood or cannot understand customers. Added to this is a detachment from local culture and geography, all of which means that overseas call centre personnel are ill equipped to adequately manage customer issues – problems go unresolved and frustrations are heightened.

Just as bad as overseas contact centres and automated responses are voicemails. This is when you call up someone (at their office, on a land line) and you get their answer phone message – why is that? Why wouldn't you just route your telephone to someone else in the office, a real person that can have a real conversation with the customer. If I want to talk with someone and I get a voicemail I have to disconnect the call and find another number to call back on, it's all extra hassle I could do without.

What does your customer want when they call your office? They want to speak with someone that's going to answer their question or deal with their enquiry – why do we make it so hard to get this?

Understanding and managing your customers' expectations

Managing your customers' expectations is absolutely essential for creating a great customer experience. Let me share with you a very simple example of what I mean.

Many moons ago when working in the hospitality industry I developed a process called 'Positive Queuing'. You see one evening I was watching the behaviour of the customers in the bar we owned right in the depths of a busy Friday night. The bar was three or four deep with customers waiting to be served, which in itself wasn't good, but we were a popular spot and we couldn't get any more staff behind the bar, so what were we to do?.

Now I had seen this sort of behaviour before but had never actually analysed it – most of the customers actually standing at the bar were holding their £20 notes way out in front of themselves in an obvious attempt to attract some service. It wasn't just this that stood out – I could see that these customers were unhappy, perhaps even stressed and that was something I didn't want for my customers. It was clear to me that this wasn't a good experience.

But what could I do? We were trading at capacity, short of turning people away they were just going to have to wait. OK – so I couldn't change the circumstances but I could educate my customers that in busy times there would be a short wait – how was I to do this?

So, after a little thought I came up with the idea of Positive Queuing and I instructed my staff the very next day what I wanted them to do. As soon as the bar got busy, I wanted them to acknowledge everybody that approached the bar so that the customers knew we had seen them. I then told them to make it clear to the customers who they were going to serve now and on what order they would serve the others. Something along the lines of, "Hi, I'm just going to serve this guy now, after that this lady who has been waiting for a while and I'm going to come to you right after."

The effect was as dramatic as it was instant!

That evening things couldn't have been different to the night before. We were busy again but instead of fretful faces at the bar waving £20 notes around, all I could see were happy faces. My customers now knew that they would have a

15

short wait but they also know at what point they were going to be served. So instead of wasting valuable enjoyment time trying to attract the attention of the barman, they turned back to chat with their friends confident in the knowledge that the barman would come to them in good time as promised.

This is a great illustration of how managing customers' expectations can be so simple.

The effect of this action is stark because it manages the customers' expectation and because it takes account of the fact that as a species we subconsciously anticipate the outcomes of every action we take. We create a mind map, an expectation of what we think will result from the actions we take – let me show you.

Let's assume that this evening you are going to have sausages for tea (stick with me on this even if you don't like sausages) – the thing is your fridge is bare and so you're going to need to go out and buy some sausages to fulfil your desires.

Now – you probably haven't given this much thought but my guess is that you will already know exactly where and how you're going to buy those sausages. This is because you already have a fixed map in your mind of how buying sausages is going to go. You have a fixed set of expectations based on previous experiences. Let's explore:

Some of you will be able to walk to the local store, others will have a short drive. When you get to the store you'll walk to the appropriate counter, pick up your sausages and take them to the checkout – pay, leave and go home. Easy right?

But your mental mind map, your expectation of buying sausages doesn't make provision for anything out of the ordinary or in fact anything other than a flawless buying experience – consider the following, where any number of issues can spoil your expectations:

- You get in your car and you don't have enough fuel or if you're walking it's raining and you don't have an umbrella.
- You stop for fuel on the way- its busy, you have to queue.
- You arrive at the supermarket and you can't park where you normally park (that stretch of spaces right next to the entrance) so you have to

park elsewhere but only after five minutes of driving around and around until you find one.

- You get in the supermarket but there are no baskets – you have to walk to the nearest till to take one from there.
- You walk through a busier than normal store, which means lots of people in the way.
- When you get to the meat aisle they've moved everything around and the sausages are somewhere else entirely.
- You look around for five minutes before giving up on finding them and search out the nearest assistant.
- The assistant walks you straight to the right place (that's a good thing) but when you get there the shelf is bare.
- Your assistant has wondered off so you can't ask them to go and look for more out back – you choose a brand you haven't had before, you're not sure but you're hungry.
- You pick up the pack of sausages to put in your basket and the packaging is sticky with raw sausage stickiness – you wipe your hand on your trousers because there's nowhere else. They need to go in the wash when you get back.
- You get to the check out but as I said the store is busier than normal so there's a big queue – you have to wait in line but guess what your line is the slowest – the guy in front has an 'unexpected item in the packing area'.
- You scan your sausages but when you go to pay for them you realise that you don't have any cash – you were going to get some from the cashpoint when you came in but you forgot.
- You get your credit card out and pay for your sausages – you don't want a bag (you only have the sausages) but the self service checkout won't let you go unless you put your sausages in a bag in the packing area – you take the bag and your receipt and you leave.
- You get outside and it's raining – you didn't bring an umbrella and you had to park way across the car park so you're going to get wet.
- You get in the car and just to be kind you have an uneventful journey home.

By the way – you didn't even enjoy the sausages; they weren't your normal brand.

It's easy to see how any one or two of these events happening can take the shine off my expected experience but imagine how I would feel if all of the above instances actually occurred. I guess I wouldn't be in the best of moods and I'm quite sure that the supermarket would be taking the brunt of my angst.

Let me put it another way – just to meet my expectations (not even to exceed them) but just to give me an experience that I am expecting none of these negative occurrences must happen. It just shows how high our expectations are when simply buying sausages.

There are several points here that we need to understand if we are to develop our own businesses. Firstly, meeting your customer's expectation, hard though that may be, just isn't enough, I can go and buy sausages anywhere and get the same experience. If you want to build loyal, delighted customers you have to exceed their expectations. Now that may be easier than you might first expect.

Exceeding expectations is certainly difficult if your customers have high expectations in the first place but as I've shown you above customers' expectations of your business are extremely wide and varied. The sausage example shows us that nicely. So the key here is pick up on the areas of least expectation and look at how you might be able to do something out of the ordinary. Let me give you an example:

I have a client who up until quite recently ran a nice hotel/catering facility on the outskirts of Bristol. Today they are a premier eating out location with a very high profile brand but earlier on they weren't quite so prestigious. So at the outset of our relationship I had certain expectations of the level and quality of food I could expect in their dining area. I expected it to be OK and very much in line with many, many other catering establishments I had visited on many, many occasions – that is to say nothing to write home about but it filled a hole.

In particular I have this thing about chips! On the whole most foodie pubs and middle of the road dining establishments buy bulk ready prepared chips that just need to go in the oven or fryer for a few minutes before being ready to serve. You'll be familiar with the sort of thing I mean, they're the long flat chips that you've no doubt had hundreds of times before.

So here I am at one of the very first meetings I have had with this new client and I have been invited to have some lunch with them, which included a bowl of chips to share. Imagine my delight when a short time later our food arrived including a large bowl of the most delicious looking and tasting chips I had had in a very long time. Perfectly cut, long and square and deliciously golden brown as if they had been roasted and not fried at all – and they tasted fabulous.

It turns out that my client served only triple cooked chips! After carefully cutting the chips by hand, they would first blanche them in boiling water, then fry them until golden before storing them in the fridge and frying them for a second time before serving – end result, fabulous chips!

The point here is that my expectations when it came to something as simple as a bowl of chips were not very high at all. So when I was presented with something that totally smashed my expectation I instantly became engaged with the business and my experience is now one of delight! My client, Cadbury House near Bristol now runs the prestigious Marco Pierre White Grill, which shows how much they have developed in such a short while. If you're ever near there you should try it, the chips are great!

So as business people I hope that you can see that exceeding your customers' expectations needn't be a monumental task, nor does it need to be an expensive one. I hope you can also see from our little sausage exercise that there are countless opportunities to really excel if we think about what actually constitutes the whole customer experience when they deal with you.

The fact that I have recounted this tale to you shows the impact of something as simple as really great chips. It's stuck in my mind and is the highpoint of my experience. So much so that I don't even remember what else I had to eat! Nevertheless, don't get fooled into thinking that if you deliver one aspect of your service exceptionally well that you will have got it made – you haven't. On its own really great chips won't mask serious deficiencies elsewhere. In fact fabulous chips will soon be forgotten if everything else is a shambles.

Don't forget the sausage exercise shows us that the customer experience is made up of a vast number of mini-expectations that form an overall experience. Some of these will be beyond your capacity to influence and some just too difficult to influence but many give you the opportunity to excel without great cost.

When we first looked at the sausage exercise we listed out how we thought buying a pack of sausages would go and we achieved this in just a few short lines.

It wasn't until we really started to analyse it that we discovered how complex the experience actually was. Our minds park-up the non-essential elements of our sausage buying experience and relegate them to mere subconscious acknowledgement. We don't consciously think about whether or not we can park where we want to, or that the shelves have been re-arranged. Nevertheless these things subconsciously impact on our appreciation, or not, of the experience.

This is proved out time and time again through the work we do helping our clients manage their customer feedback. One of the principle functions for our clients is to ensure that they always respond to a customer that's given them feedback – good, bad or indifferent. The objective here is to either thank them for the great feedback or remedy any issues that the customer might have. I am constantly challenged by client management teams who continuously argue that when they contact a customer that has given them an indifferent score, the customer can't be specific about what they could have done better. Their point is that if the customer can't specifically identify anything wrong or unsatisfactory then surely the customer is a happy one – wrong!

Customers don't consciously analyse their experience – there's too much going on for them to be really bothered about it but their subconscious does pick up on things that don't meet expectation. So when a customer gives you a mediocre score they're probably not sure why they have done so – it just feels right for the experience they have had. We'll talk more on this later in this book.

So if we really want to give our customers a great experience, we need to:

- Look at the whole customer experience in every elemental detail:
    ° Think about what the customer sees and feels when they interact with you
    ° Where does this interaction start and end, and what are the touch points in between
- Find as many ways as we can to excel against the customer's expectation:
    ° Do this with lots of little things – not just one big statement
    ° This doesn't mean spend lots of money – it just means doing the basics really well
- Make all of this show the customer that we value their business:
    ° More on this later!

Finally – don't make the mistake of thinking your customers are different to

other customers. That they're somehow more refined or behave differently, or that where you operate customers are different to everywhere else.
That's rubbish and is often used as an excuse for poor performance or feedback.

All customers are humans (they are!) and all humans inherently have the same fundamental psychology, whether they're buying a Mars bar or a Porsche. The only difference between customers is the level of their expectation.

When I visit Porsche to buy a car I'm investing a huge amount of money and with that I have a high expectation on how the experience will go. I'm expecting very attentive staff in pleasant if not ostentatious surroundings. I expect this partly because Porsche (and other motor manufacturers) have led me to believe that is what I should expect and partly because I am paying for it. On the other hand, when I buy a Mars bar I have very little expectation because you get what you pay for and my Mars bar is only a few pence. But do you seriously expect a Porsche buyer to have any more an expectation about buying a Mars bar than anyone else – of course not.

I work with very many professional service companies who prefer to call their customers 'clients'. Now that's ok if they're using this title to reflect a degree of professionalism but not if they think that their clients are different to anyone else's customers – they're not!

So here's the thing – all customers are the same. They all intrinsically go through the same fundamental processes when they interact with businesses they want to buy from. This is good news because it means whatever your business, whatever products and services you provide, you will learn all the skills you need in this book to deliver a really fabulous customer experience. Customers are customers, the only thing that ever changes is the level of expectation.

Having a 'Heads Up' culture

This is all about the customer and their experience as absolutely nothing is more important than serving the customer. Many years ago when I first started out in my career I was lucky enough to work in a small town insurance brokerage, which grew into the UK's biggest consumer durable warranty specialist in a matter of just a few short years.

I had been working with a great friend of mine Kerry Michael, now owner of the spectacular Grand Pier in Weston-super-Mare, and together we managed the most successful pub in the region by miles, the fabled Imp that I have referred to previously. Inevitably sooner or later he was going to be made an offer he couldn't refuse and eventually he sold it. At that time he had an interest in a local insurance brokerage and decided to see if he could make a go of it in the insurance industry and invited me along with him.

Straight away it wasn't difficult to see where the problems were. Like many traditional insurance broker businesses at that time customers were separated from the staff by means of an elongated counter, which served as an effective barrier to customer service. The staff would spend much of their day carrying out the many paperwork duties that formed their job function. Every now and then this was punctuated by the odd customer that walked through the door. Their reaction to this customer was startling. At the sound of the door handle they would all in unison bow their heads forward and engage furiously in whatever task it was that they were doing, actively discouraging the customer as much as they could from approaching their own particular station.

Let me quash another myth for you, customers are not stupid! Any customer entering the brokerage at that time would have unquestionably felt ignored and perhaps even unwanted. And indeed they were. The staff saw the customer not as the pivotal element in the success of the business, but as an interruption to the administrative work they were required to do. Whether it occurred to them that without any customers there would be no paperwork to administer I am unsure. Nevertheless their attitude (through deliberate action or sheer stupidity) stank and customers were all too aware of it. But why did the staff behave this way, what could have caused such a massive shift in focus away from the customer? Sadly, the answer is all too obvious. Poor business culture, misguided staff and weak management had resulted in a slow decaying of the customer focus.

It wasn't long before Kerry had torn down the counter and re-organised the regime in such a way that customers coming through the door took priority above all else. It was this change in customer focus that ultimately led to his business becoming one of the most successful businesses of its time. Now when you enter the very same offices the sound of the door handle is a welcome one and all the staff look up eagerly, each keen to be the one to serve the customer and it's this change in culture that I have called 'Heads Up', where the customer takes priority.

Heads Up is about prioritising the customer above all else. This can be very challenging for some businesses and individuals who have become lackadaisical about customer service during the immensely profitable good times and entirely process driven as a consequence, which will be the subject of our next chapter.

So what are we saying here? Well listen, I'm going to tell you something that will revolutionise the way you work within your business and change the way you do things forever! Your business is not about whatever it is you do or sell, it's about looking after your customers and the experience that gives them. Let's make this clear, everything you do, every process you adopt should be geared to exceeding your customers' needs and giving outstanding service. As long as you always work towards your customers delight you will build a reputation for excellence and you will always be successful.

And just to be doubly sure, I'm going to give a simple statement that absolutely everybody within your organisation (including you) should learn by heart and put into practice all day every day.

"There is no action, function or process that is more important or takes precedent over serving the customer".

You really have to get behind this and make it part of your business psyche, it will make your business stand out.

Quite often I get pulled up on this one, normally by the managing director or CEO, someone quite highly ranked within an organisation who has come to believe that there are many things they do that are essential to the successful running of the business.

I'm certainly not detracting from the work they do but I am saying that serving the customer is more important. You see customers don't know (or care) about the individuals within an organisation or their specific roles within it. All they see is a member of staff who should be serving them.

This is particularly prevalent in businesses that have different teams of individuals to serve different types of customer. The motor industry is certainly one that comes to mind, where staff are designated as 'sales' or 'service' staff. Customers of course won't see or appreciate any difference between these two sets of staff and will become intensely irritated if they feel that they are being ignored by someone who appears on the face of it to be able to serve them. They don't see that these individuals work in a different department and even if they did, they wouldn't accept this as an excuse to ignore them.

So it comes down to this, if you really want to give your customers an outstanding customer experience then you need to ensure that every member of your staff is capable of interacting with a customer even if it's at a very basic level. And if you are the CEO of a large organisation what better way to demonstrate the importance of the customer in your company than by serving them yourself. Imagine the impact on your customers and your personal and business reputation. Let me tell you that all the most successful people I know would never pass by a customer that needed serving.

Lost in process – the hardest habit to break

The lines between business process and customer service are often blurred.

Process in business is absolutely essential. It defines people's roles, maintains continuity of supply and ensures product/service fulfilment. It controls expenditure and provides the entire framework around which a business operates. Whether you're a big business or a small café, process governs the way you do things. It determines what time you open, how many staff you have and, for many of you, the way in which you deliver your product or service, and the extent of your customer service.

Not everyone naturally and instinctively knows and understands how to care for their customers. Generally business leaders and owners have a disposition for this sort of thing, which is probably why they have attained their position of success. But that doesn't mean that they always get it right. This book is full of personal accounts that show how easy it is for businesses to get it wrong. Harder still, the ability of big companies to take the great intentions at board level and deliver them on the shop floor.

This is because the intentions and good will of the senior managers is often diluted by the time it has cascaded through several lines of middle management, before it finally reaches the front end customer-facing staff. And here we are again, just as we started this book, talking about the lack of training, support and resources given to the most important people in any business – the people that deal with the customers – they are the company's face and the company will be judged on how well they perform in their role.

But business doesn't get all the blame for bad service, poor performing staff must also take their fair share of the blame. Front end customer facing staff that don't perform as they should do so for only one of three reasons:

- They're stupid
- They're lazy
- They don't give a damn.

I have borrowed these three reasons from a guy called Larry Wingett, a self help guru who uses these descriptions to demonstrate why people don't attain success. I believe they have a much broader application including our ability to pretty much achieve anything we do.

If we take them in the context of delivering good customer service and apply them to rubbish customer service experiences, we can see how they work.

They're stupid – refers to ignorance or lack of understanding on how to deliver great customer service or why. This is probably because they haven't had sufficient training to do their job well or perhaps the company they work for thinks that their function is so menial that it doesn't warrant training (and that's really stupid). This also applies to those people that think that the process is more important – these are the people that finish what they're doing before making the effort to serve us.

They're lazy – this is for me the most common reason why we get rubbish customer service. Staff have become accustomed to a slow pace of work with prolonged periods of inactivity and find it hard to motivate themselves to sometimes even ask the customer if they would like any assistance. We talk more about this phenomenon later.

They don't give a damn – sadly there are some people out there that just don't care whether or not they give good customer service. In fact they don't care whether or not they do any aspect of their job well. These people may well be transient, already minded to work elsewhere or they may just be so poorly managed that they are allowed to behave in this way. Perhaps they think that they're not being paid enough to warrant the effort – sorry that doesn't wash for me. If you don't like the job – LEAVE! If you don't you will soon find yourself being fired – and well deserved too!

These three things are a reflection on the customer service culture a company has and it's this culture that defines the experience we have as customers when we interact with a company. It's hard to give good examples of well-known companies where a business culture has been developed that is reflected in its company service and therefore in its reputation.

John Lewis springs to mind as a company that's principal business structure drives good customer service through a culture of ownership – a collective of partners who all benefit from the success of the company. But it's the ownership element that creates the culture here. I can only think of one company I have come across that has a culture for great customer service for the sake of it and that's Apple. The Apple store is filled with employees that are not only engaged with the company and its products, but also with the customer. I find them incredibly attentive, helpful and engaging and have not yet had a bad experience. However, in all my experience they are the only ones. I can't think of any others.

This is because on the whole customer service is 'just another' process devised by the company when in fact customer service should not be a process at all. It should be a culture, done because it was the right and proper thing to do not because somewhere some rule book demands it. Rules and processes come about because of a lack of customer service culture – they are devised to counteract the lack of culture but this is the wrong approach as they only serve to produce a sterile process, which is insincere and recognised as such. So when the girl from TGI Fridays tells you to have a nice day, you know that she really doesn't mean it and probably couldn't care less whether or not it turns out that way.

So the best way to deal with poor customer service isn't through process, it's through culture – and that's a whole other chapter.

What's important here and the principal reason for this chapter is to illustrate that when you make customer service just another process it gets lost in all the other business processes and has no more nor or less importance and that's a real problem because customer service should take precedence over everything else a member of your staff does.

So we're saying that customer service shouldn't be a sterile process and that it should be personal, genuine and warm and that this is really achieved when our staff believe and take pride in what they do – ownership.

So what does this mean, what is the purpose then of all the processes we put into our company? well for me this is really straightforward and is a key part of the work we do with our clients – ask yourself this simple question about every process you have in your business: "Does this process enhance or detract from my customers' experience?"

Business processes should be devised and implemented for the sole reason of delivering a great customer experience and that's how they normally start. Problem is that long-term we lose sight of this goal and we find ourselves developing more and more processes (many in support of other processes) without considering the impact on the customer experience.

This is the start of the downward slide, when a new process is suddenly implemented without consideration to the customer experience it becomes ring fenced from it – immune from the negative effects on the customer, a law unto itself. The shift in focus doesn't go unnoticed by staff, who no longer have to consider the impact of what they do on the customer – the process becomes their 'raison d'être', their purpose of employment and the object of their attention.

Ladies and gentlemen, I introduce you to the 'jobsworth'.

This is a great term, originally coined in the 1980s and taken from a TV programme called 'That's Life', where the hostess at the time (Esther Rantzen, for those of you that remember it) would use the term to describe people so ludicrously process orientated that they would often disregard all sense and reason to blindly follow prescribed directions. These people were so called because they refused to be persuaded with reason, quite often citing that it was "more than their job's worth" to behave otherwise.

These people aren't employed, businesses don't recruit them – they create them! They take normal reasonably competent individuals and indoctrinate them with so much process that they are unable to see beyond to the bigger picture. These people exist because businesses allow them to.

So if we want to avoid the traps that lead to jobworths in our business we have to ensure that we understand the purpose of our processes.

Your company processes, as vast as they may be, exist to serve only one purpose – to support or enhance the customer experience. If they can't achieve this, get rid of them or change them!

OK this is a biggy! A huge statement to make, and even harder to achieve, sometimes impossible, let me explain. I work a lot with businesses in the motor industry and have some pretty nifty motor dealer clients that have an absolutely fabulous approach to their customers – and left to their own devises they would be able to achieve monumental successes. However, they are confined by the motor manufacturers they deal with to operate in commercial ways that have no bearing on the customer experience.

The biggest driver for motor manufacturers isn't the customers' experience, it's the number of cars they sell. Now, that's OK, they're commercial enterprises and they have a duty to deliver dividends to their shareholders, and their driver is unit sales. Now I don't agree with this approach, but I understand it — for me delivering a fabulous customer experience ultimately leads to fabulous sales figures, the two go hand-in-hand (assuming that you have a good product to start with — but that's for later).

But motor manufacturers don't see this — they see an unshakeable, immovable target of vehicle sales each month that they are fanatically obsessive about. This obsession disseminates itself into their dealer network as immense pressure to bring forward as many sales as possible into the month of trade. This often manifests itself in onward pressure on customers to take delivery, and sometimes pay for cars, well before they had planned to.

This isn't good.

In fact it's unnecessary. Does it really matter whether a car is invoiced today or tomorrow? Well for the motor manufacturer it does — for them it's all about the numbers each month. If only they would obsess about the customer experience in the same way! This is short-term-ism, I know of businesses that work in this way who simply don't exist beyond the end of this month. That is to say that they have no interest in anything that occurs outside of the month they're in — nothing else matters than the here and now. With such a short-term view they will make no provision for repeat business, referrals or customer retention, these factors simply don't matter when you are only interested in this month's figures.

Not surprising that these businesses have little or no affinity with their customers, who generally only buy from them on price-related deals (often the only compensation for the lack of service). This in turn puts pressure on margins and profits, which in turn pushes business focus on even more and more unit sales — and so the whole downward spiral goes on.

So we can see that the desire to hit the numbers can be at direct odds to the need to give the customer a great experience and despite how focused my motor dealer clients are on delivering great customer service, exterior pressures and constraints are sometimes unavoidable. All you can do in these circumstances is manage as best as possible and maintain as strong a focus as possible on delivering a great customer experience.

My best clients know this, and despite the inward pressures they receive they realise that the long-term game is more important. In the motor industry this means building your own reputation as a great customer focused dealer, rather than riding on the back of the manufacturer whose cars they sell.

So you can see that even the world's most successful companies can find themselves victims of a misaligned orientation towards their processes.

So who makes your reputation?

This is a question I often ask my clients and their staff and one which attracts almost always the same response:

"We do!"

"OK," I reply, "Who else?"

"Er..., our customers."

"Yep, who else?"

It's usually at this point I get a lot of scratching of heads and blank faces. This is because most of us can't see beyond our sphere of immediate influence – we can affect our behaviour and the behaviour of our staff, and we can affect the experience we give our customers. But beyond that it's not clear what else impacts on our reputation.

And it's an interesting question: "who makes our reputation?" with an even more interesting answer – anyone that cares to have an opinion!

It's an amalgam of opinions that establish a business' reputation, a melting pot of different experiences, prejudices, overheard conversations and hearsay that combine to form a general underlying feeling towards a company.

Anyone can have an opinion and most of us do! And that opinion does not need to be based on factual evidence or personal experience – it's an opinion. Google defines the word 'opinion' as: a personal belief or judgment that is not founded on proof or certainty.

This definition sums it up nicely – and helps us to understand how opinions are formed, both good and bad.

My chum Frank, while sitting in the pub one evening enjoying a pint with the locals, chanced to hear upon a conversation about a local fish and chip shop. "Oh, you don't want to go there," says Frank, "my Dad went there and they were rubbish."

And so there you have it! An opinion expressed, based on nothing other than hearsay, which has a direct influence on those within earshot. But why can opinions be so influential?

Opinions both good and bad are given freely (sometimes too freely!) without any desire for personal gain. Most are based on real experiences if not the direct experiences of those individuals holding them. Beyond that opinion can reflect fashionable viewpoints and even cultural differences – there is a whole science here, most of which is probably too intricate for us to concern ourselves with.

The key for us is that everyone can have an opinion and that means that everyone that comes into contact with you and your business will have an opinion about it – what's important is what you do to make it a positive one.

Equally you should be highly aware just who 'everyone' is:

- You
- Your staff
- Your customers
- The people that supply you
- The people that walk by you
- The people that deliver to you
- The people in the buildings next to you
- The people that are 'just looking'.

It really is everybody!

When you look at it in this light you can see how every aspect of your business has a direct effect on those people whose opinions directly make up your business reputation. How many of you make the effort to engage the hoards of delivery drivers that bring supplies to your company every day? How many of you invest the same effort into customers that are 'just looking' as you do in your regular customers?

It's perhaps an appropriate moment to tell you about a phrase used very often in the car sales industry. It's a derogatory term reserved for a group of people called 'tyre kickers'. It will help me to explain perfectly the danger of not considering your reputation in everything that you do.

You see 'tyre kickers' is a very short-sighted term adopted by car sales professionals (if I can call them that) to describe those individuals that visit their car showroom without the express intent of purchasing a vehicle. It's derived from the actions of those visitors, that when inspecting a vehicle, would often kick its tyres as if to establish their roadworthiness. It's used to define someone who is effectively considered to be a time waster and it's a dangerously flawed prejudice, let me explain.

For starters, I do not believe for one moment that anyone visiting a car showroom is just on a day out. I can think of a million things I would rather do and enjoy more than visiting a car showroom, so as far as I am concerned anyone visiting your business does so with at least some small amount of interest. This may not be for a purchase now but nonetheless a purchase is certainly in mind at some point.

But let's just say for the purposes of this argument that we have a visitor who has no intention to buy, not now, not ever – does this mean that we should treat them as an irritation, an obstacle to dealing with 'real' customers? To which the answer can only be unequivocally: "no".

We have the opportunity with everybody that interacts with our business to develop our reputation or tarnish it. For me it is quite simple, whoever visits my car showroom is guaranteed a great customer experience, whether they came to buy that day or not. This is because I recognise that I have the perfect opportunity to establish a rapport with these individuals and the perfect opportunity to send them away thinking that my business is absolutely fantastic.

I invest as much time with these individuals as I do with all of my customers, even though I recognise that they won't necessarily be purchasing from me today. I also know that my investment will pay dividends as I increase the number of positive advocates for my business. What is a stronger positive advocate than someone who received an excellent level of service even though it was clear they weren't an immediate purchaser.

Let me put this the other way around – let's just say that I simply cannot be bothered with these 'tyre kickers', I give them the bums rush, ignore them at best and at worst make it absolutely clear I have no interest in them. What impact does this have on my reputation? What impact can this have on my sales? Let's explore this thought.

Think about all the people you know.

Let's take your immediate family, your parents, children, uncles, aunts, cousins, nephews and nieces. How many people in your immediate family? For me this is more than 50 people (although perhaps expected with an Italian background) and that's just my immediate family.

What about your friends, the people you socially interact with? Well I have to say I am blessed with very many wonderful people that I am fortunate enough to be able to call friends. Nowadays of course, with the advent of social media (Facebook, Myspace and so on) we find ourselves with a great many more friends/ acquaintances than we could have ever imagined. For me again this is close to 50 people that I can call friends rather than acquaintances.

And then of course there are the people I work with, not just my immediate colleagues but the other people I interact with every day carrying out my professional duties – my suppliers, my customers and so on. How many people here do I engage with on a daily basis? Twenty, maybe thirty – you may have many more.

Of course the point here is to get some form of idea of exactly the sphere of influence each of us has on the people around us. For me that's approaching 140 people, all of whom would value my opinion and be influenced by it. So if I look at this commercially, investing in a 'tyre kicker' is allowing me to influence as many as 140 other individuals, establishing a reputation for customer service excellence that will at some point in time pay a return on my investment. Or not – the choice is yours.

In truth, if we want to develop an outstanding business reputation we should invest time and energy into all of the people that touch our business – ensuring that no-one walks away not having at least experienced some warmth from their interaction.

There is a simple technique you can use to help you in part achieve this, sadly not one I can claim for myself but nonetheless a super bit of thinking from a great mind somewhere – it's called the '10ft Rule'.

The 10ft Rules says that you have to smile and acknowledge anyone that comes to within 10ft of you – easy! The 10ft Rule isn't restricted just to customers or fellow staff members it's for everyone and anyone – if someone comes within 10ft, you smile and acknowledge them. It's so simple yet its impact can be incredible – if enforced correctly it ensures that everyone that touches your business is, at the very least, assured a pleasant welcome.

This is only the start, the 10ft Rule in itself brings about a state of mind, a way of thinking that happens almost by accident – it's well-known that by disciplining yourself to smile regularly in this way actually improves your mood. So you see by adopting and enforcing the 10ft Rule we find ourselves lifting the ambience of our business, making it more welcoming and generally a more pleasant place to be.

Of course the 10ft Rule on its own isn't enough to establish your business' reputation but it will certainly help. In truth, your reputation is established on a whole host of factors, not least of which is the purchase and post purchase experience you give your customer and these are the factors that we are examining in this book.

Being 'customer centric'

'Customer centric' is one of those new fluffy buzz phrases picked up by large corporations. It's a phrase used to describe a level of service that treats each customer as a unique individual, with their own individual wants and needs. Now this is easy if you're a small local business with a good regular customer base that you are able to nurture on a day-by-day basis, but try achieving the same level of service with a national business with multiple outlets, let me explain...

In Weston-super-Mare, a well-known seaside town close to where I live, there exists to this day a Chinese restaurant owned by a man whose ability to be customer centric has in my eyes never been surpassed. He had the unique ability to remember people's names and faces, so much so that once you had visited his restaurant once or twice he would remember you by name and if you should become a frequent visitor he would even remember your favourite dishes from the menu. He welcomed all his customers personally, taking the time to speak with them all. He remembered small details like what they did for a living, how many children they had or where they went on holiday and, in particular, he knew where they liked to sit and what they liked to eat.

So congenial was he with this that his restaurant soon became very popular and grew from strength-to-strength expanding upwards and outwards to accommodate the ever increasing demand for tables. Such was its success that he expanded his business empire into other areas. As his success continued these other interests demanded more and more of his time until eventually he no longer stood front of house in his restaurant. Perhaps as to be expected the restaurant declined a little, it was still very popular but without the man behind the wheel and his unique customer centric approach, it became no different to any other restaurant.

The fact is, as an owner of a business, that no-one is ever going to look after your customers as well as you do and that when you're not there things just aren't going to be the same. This is a problem of ownership, the owner of a business has a vested interest in its success and goes out of the way to consolidate his customer base through good customer service. Whereas other staff, more often than not, have nothing to gain from the additional effort. Now compound this situation and imagine that you own not one business but three or four, how can you possibly spread yourself around all three to the extent that you're making a positive effect on the customer experience at each location?

It is here where we see large corporations setting out more and more defined rules as to how you should approach the customer, what you should say and what you should do, so prescribed are some of these functions that they become parrot-like and insincere. Customers recognise this, after all they're not stupid. When I'm told to "have a nice day", do I really believe that this person sincerely cares whether or not I do?

As I said earlier on, fundamentally this is a problem of ownership – not necessarily ownership of the business but ownership of the customer and ownership of the customer's experience. Of course not every business is the same and there are some excellent professional hosts out there that do an exceptional job because they take pride in themselves and the work they do. It incenses me when I hear about businesses that don't reward their staff properly for good customer service or worse still actively steal the tips that were meant for the professional host.

Some months ago I visited an upmarket Italian restaurant in the heart of Bristol that was part of a well-known national chain. The host was excellent and took great care to ensure that our experience was a good one. As we should all do, I left him a good tip that reflected the hard work he had invested in us. As it was a business lunch, I paid for the meal and his tip using my credit card.

Such was the level of service I had from this particular individual that I found myself using the restaurant more frequently. One day, out of the blue, the gentleman that had served me so well handed me my bill and explained in a quite hushed manner that he thanked me for my regular custom, but thought I should know, that when paying by credit card the company kept all the tips. He had deliberately waited until my colleague had left the table so as not to cause any more embarrassment than was necessary and was clearly uncomfortable making me aware of the situation. I thanked him for letting me know and from then on always made sure that I had cash enough to tip him whenever I visited that restaurant again.

I have to say I was astonished and outraged at such abysmal behaviour and have since learned that this was quite normal behaviour for large chain restaurants. In fact you might recall that there was a big exposé on this very subject and many companies have since changed their policy. Now, as far as the restaurant was concerned I could have illustrated my disgust by refusing to dine there anymore but the food was good and the service great. Moreover moving my custom elsewhere wasn't exactly going to make things better for my professional host. So I continued to eat there and if, like me, you feel that you would like to leave a tip to any professional host that has served you well, please always enquire as to who actually benefits from your gratitude.

Of course professional hosts that work in an environment where the public are able to reflect their appreciation through tipping are at an advantage. There are many businesses and professions that serve the customer where no such expectation exists. Shop workers, check-in staff, public service and call centre personnel all provide a service to the public but are unlikely to receive tips. It is even more important here that such individuals are rewarded through a pay scheme that takes account of customer satisfaction, so that the greater the satisfaction, the greater the rewards.

But I would like to suggest a more radical approach to tipping, one that is much simpler – I believe that tipping should be abolished altogether!

Whoa, I can just hear the anguished cries of tens of thousands of individuals who work really hard for their tips, without which life would be much harder, but hear me out here…

For me the problems are straight forward, for starters waiting staff are just not paid enough for the work they do. This in itself denigrates the value of their role and gives the impression that waiting staff are not valued as individuals or professionals.

As I've said before this seems to be complete madness to me! These people are the face of the company, the individuals with whom we as customers have a direct relationship and on whom we base much of our experience with the company. Yet still we seek to employ low skilled individuals for this job on the lowest of rewards.

It's hardly surprising then that many waiting or service staff are discontented with their job and often treat it as a stop gap or temporary arrangement, constantly on the lookout for alternative employment. Hardly the level of loyalty companies look for in their most important resource – their staff! And it's this denigration of the service role that leads all individuals, both employers and employees, to treat it with contempt. Enthusiasm for giving good customer service at the coal face is often driven by process more than by desire, or stick rather than carrot if you prefer.

The lack of respect for waiting and service staff is driven by the mistaken belief that no special skills are required to hold down such a role – this is wrong as we will see later in this book. However, it seems to be the norm to provide very little training to new recruits other than functional, by which I mean how to work the till, how to set the tables or how to write down an order. Generally, these functions are undertaken adequately but don't contribute much to the overall customer experience.

Poor inadequate training shows little regard for the role on the part of the employer and this is often carried through by waiting staff, many of whom have little pride in the standard or work they do.

The role has descended to that of a commodity, a function that anyone can do – an unskilled job that attracts low remuneration – after all if you don't want the job, there are hundreds that do. An air of expendability permeates throughout the service industry and companies build their business models with the expectation of a high staff turnover.

Sadly, there are a few cherished individuals who really do love their job and want to be just fantastic at giving service. Yet these people never get the exposure they deserve and whom often start out brimming with enthusiasm only to be brow beaten and chided into providing the same poor service as the rest.

So when you think about it the whole system is broken and dysfunctional. Instead of a model that looks for constant improvement we have a model that looks for constant cost reductions.

Yet a change of approach might just be what this industry needs. Perhaps one or two highly focused companies that are really driven on building a team of professional service personnel. A team that is supported with extensive, in depth training and whose function is to provide attentive (but not stuffy) service. A team that takes great pride in the work they do and the level of skill they achieve.

These staff would enjoy the work they do and take pride in the results they bring. Such is their level of expertise, that they demand a level of payment that is way above anyone else in their sector – and their employers are happy to pay. They're happy because their business standards are recognised as among the very best. They're happy because their customers come back to them time and time again, and they're happy because their market share grows daily at the expense of their mediocre competition

Staff turnover is all but non-existent, as are recruitment costs. Personnel love the work they do, enjoy their hard earned rewards and are loyal to their employers. Customers become positive advocates, will be less sensitive to price and will buy more and more often. Sure it costs more – but the results speak for themselves.

So I propose to abolish tips in favour of a pay structure that reflects the importance of this job as the key customer facing role – let's pay properly and demand good quality, consistent service. Tips should not be the method employed by companies to generate good customer service – this should be down to pride.

Right now, particularly in these service sectors, the level of customer service offered is generally atrocious. This is because staff are not given any ownership for customer service. To them it makes no difference whether or not they smile at the customer or use simple courtesies like "hello", "thank you" and "goodbye", in fact the customer is often considered to be that same hindrance we observed earlier on in this book, especially during quieter times – which I will cover later. Consequently, those customers that do venture into these businesses are likely to find that their presence feels less than welcome.

In fact, here is a little experiment for you that I have conducted myself on a number of occasions. Next time you go out shopping see if you can make a simple purchase, say a newspaper, a loaf of bread or some batteries, anything that you can pick up yourself from a shelf and take to the checkout and see if you can conclude your purchase without either the cashier or yourself exchanging any of the common courtesies such as "hello", "goodbye", "please" or "thank you". This works in some places more than others, for example a good level of training in most supermarkets means that it's unlikely you will miss a reasonable "hello". On the other hand there are numerous independent shops and national retailers where it's quite possible to do this as I have proven myself on a number of occasions.

Now, you might argue that the cashier won't show the customer these simple courtesies if they themselves aren't offered the same. But let's not forget here that these staff are being paid to service the customer. This function will require them to act courteously regardless of whether or not the customer responds accordingly. So why do they behave in such an inappropriate manner, well there are a number of reasons some of which are listed below:

- They can't be bothered
- They are not well–managed
- They are not well–trained
- They have no ownership for customer service.

Notice that I didn't specifically mention money as a reason. This is because individuals that perform poorly in this fashion are, as far as I'm concerned, breaking the terms of their contract of employment. Nowhere in their contract will it allow them to choose where and when to be courteous or just how much effort they should put into serving customers. Such individuals are lazy and inconsiderate and should shoulder the blame equally with their managers for poor and inept service. If this is you, change your ways, start right now and if your boss doesn't appreciate you, find another one that will – high quality professional hosts are like hen's teeth and in great demand.

Unfortunately, it is sad how prevalent this attitude is within the retail and public service sectors. Some time ago I was unfortunate enough to find myself in the ASDA supermarket at Cribbs Causeway, Bristol which is now the big Walmart that you can see when heading south past Bristol on the M5. It was a Saturday and a beautiful summers day and having just finished shopping at The Mall, we decided to stop at the supermarket to get a few things for a barbeque in the garden a little later that afternoon. Not wishing to spend the whole afternoon in ASDA I scooted around as fast as I could with the family in tow close behind me. Having accumulated a good basketful of stuff, I made my way towards the checkouts.

As I rounded the corner of the aisle my jaw dropped as there in front of me for as far as the eye could see (it was a very big store) were trolleys, fully loaded and 10 deep at every checkout. It was completely conceivable that I would be spending the next hour of my life standing in line waiting to be served. It was at the point where I considered abandoning my basket of goods and making for the nearest exit when I spotted at least six (yes, count them, six) empty checkouts reserved for those customers with 10 items, or less.

Now, I knew full well that I had more than 10 items in my basket, which to be honest was rammed full, but I simply couldn't face the endless queues and after all it wasn't as if they were actually doing anything.

I turned around and made as if to head toward the nearest of the checkouts. However, when it became clear to the cashier that I was heading in her direction and bearing in mind that I was still a good 15 to 20 feet away from her, she called out in a firm tone:

"10 items or less."

That was it, nothing more just "10 items or less", no apology, no explanation not even the faintest glimmer of a smile, she just stood there arms crossed chewing on her gum, as if it was the only exercise she got.

Unfortunately, the combination of me being in a hurry and her slovenly, 'can't be bothered' attitude got my back up in an instant and the poor unfortunate cashier got a rather direct rebuke.

I pointed out to her that perhaps if the other checkouts weren't so busy I might well have queued up at the appropriately designated till and that because she wasn't actually serving anyone else what difference should it make to her serving me now. I also explained to her the importance of the customer and that she was misguided to put obstacles in the way of me handing over my cash, given that a proportion of it would ultimately end up in her wages.

She looked at me as if I was an alien and then she said:

"10 items or less."

It seems that I wasn't getting through to her and my frustration was getting the better of me and so, wishing to placate the poor unfortunate cashier I counted 10 items from my basket and placed them on the conveyor, "there you are," I said, "10 items and when you've finished them I've got another 10 items for you".

Funny as it may seem this is exactly what happened, although I was perhaps a little more forceful in my tone than I alluded to above.

I'm puzzled, how did a simple customer service policy get so out of kilter that the cashier would rather I wait a good hour or so than contravene ASDA's policy of reserving certain tills for a certain number of items, even more so when the tills in question were not even being utilised. Is it conceivable that ADSA themselves set this rule rigid? I think not. In fact I think anyone at middle management or above would have been horrified at the way in which their cashier managed the circumstance.

My experience at my local Tesco however was completely different. Here they have a different approach, in fact at my local Tesco I can take my basket of goods to any till at any point in the store. Whether it's the pharmacy or the tobacco shop, or the 10 items or less aisle. Tesco are quite happy to take my money wherever I would like to give it to them – and commercially this makes absolute sense. So Tesco operated a similar policy to that of ASDA but were able to ensure that their staff understood the importance of the customer above the importance of the traffic control and here we see the beginnings of being customer centric.

Being customer centric is the ability to be able to structure your business around the desires and the needs of your customers – easy you might think, but not so. As businesses grow they lose touch of the customer's experience front of house and their focus shifts away from the customer to bottom line profit and the processes required to deliver it. Examples of which can be found everywhere you look without any great difficulty and are particularly prevalent in major corporations despite the fact that many of them employ 'customer experience managers' to address this very issue.

The worst offenders are those corporations that feel they don't have to try – generally because they have a monopoly in their market place or close to it. Shortly before my son was born, we moved into a lovely old house that was in dire need of renovation and slowly, over a matter of months, we began to bring it into some sort of shape. One morning, while preparing the ground at the front of the house in order to put paving slabs down the workman accidentally trashed the water meter while levelling the ground with his JCB.

First off, I contacted Bristol Water and explained what had happened. I admitted that it was our fault and that we would be happy to pay for the replacement but could they get someone out right away to replace the meter as the contractors were all geared up to lay the slabs at the end of the week. I have to say, they couldn't have been more helpful. The lady I spoke with was polite, friendly and generally sympathetic to my needs. It was while we were going through the process of making the arrangements that she discovered that actually Bristol Water were only responsible for our waste and not for our water supply.

And so a few minutes later I found myself on the telephone to Wessex Water and the experience couldn't have been more different. First off, the customer service advisor I spoke with didn't sound at all like she was pleased to speak with me and was very matter of fact, almost curt with her responses. I explained again what had happened, our liability and the need for an urgent response so that my slabs could be laid at the end of the week as planned.

She asked me to put my request in writing.

Mmmmm, not a good start. I mean we've all been there, "put it in writing" actually means something like: "I can't be bothered to deal with this so if I make you put it in writing to some nameless individual it will end up on someone else's desk, a week or so from now".

It's a cop out! An abdication of responsibility, but guess what? Customers aren't stupid. "No," I explained, "that won't do." Assuming I had the determination and the time to write such a letter, I knew full well that I was extremely unlikely to receive a response to it in time for me to have my slabs laid at the end of the week.

"Why do I need to write to you? I'm here now, why can't I tell you what I need and you deal with it?" Simple enough, it wasn't hard, she was a customer service advisor and I was a customer. Her reply was one of those standard phrases the mere mention of which sends my blood boiling. A phrase so heinous that it should be consigned to the bin marked 'outdated practices that should have ceased with the dinosaurs'.

"It's not our company policy." she said.

Wow, I didn't know that there were still businesses out there archaic enough to use this phrase, apparently there was.

"Well I don't work for your company," I replied sharply, "what's your customer policy?"

Needless to say my irritation wasn't helping, but you see I just can't help

47

myself, particularly when it's more about bad attitude than bad service. A short exchange followed that resulted in me asking to speak with one of her managers, she put me on hold. A short while later she came back on the line to say that the engineers would be out the following day to fix my meter.

Success! But I still wasn't happy, why couldn't she have just done that in the first place? Worse still, I never got to speak with her manager even though I made a direct request to do so – her manager had abdicated responsibility, she copped out and made her advisor get back on the telephone to me. It was hardly surprising that their customer service advisors were so shoddy with such weak managers driving them. I didn't pursue it, I didn't need to and I didn't want to chance ruining things having just got them sorted. But you can bet your bottom dollar that for a week or two everyone I met heard all about it.

So, what's clear is that there are thousands, if not tens of thousands, of businesses out there that have absolutely no idea of what customer centric means, but there are also many more that do but find it impossible to deliver. Here's a good quote for you, its one of mine so I like it:

"To offer true customer service you must accept that each customer interaction requires a uniquely individual approach – this approach is determined by the customer and is set to their own unique agenda."

Let me explain… No two customers are ever the same, what might be acceptable to one will be unacceptable to another. They each will have their own desires and needs and to be truly customer centric you need to deal with each customer at their own level in a manner prescribed by them. It's this that mortifies big businesses – how do I get to be customer centric without massive cost for additional resources?

It's a toughie. If you want to appeal to your customer at their level then you're going to need to get down and dirty and actually engage with them. You're going to have to find out what it is they like about your business, what infuriates them, where they think you fall down and what's important to them in their relationship with you. And this by the way is not a general pattern you're looking for, not some 'lost the will to live' tick box questionnaire that you might force on your customers from time to time on the promise of a cheap meal or a weekend away. No, this is about building an individual picture of each customer, by name.

Now, there are some circumstances where this is easier to achieve than others. I mean how the hell are you going to profile a customer that walks in off the street to buy a packet of batteries? They walk in, they take a packet of batteries off the shelf, they hand them to the cashier, pay and leave. Where's the opportunity to be customer centric here? Actually plenty! First off, simple courtesies are paramount here – this customer is spending only a few minutes with you so you have a limited amount of time to make an impression. Big smiles, "hello", "please" and "thank you" are essential – the simple courtesies that make a big difference.

Remember being customer centric means letting the customer decide how much they want to engage with you. In this example this is a simple transaction, they're not looking for a meaningful conversation here – they want in and out as soon as possible. Being customer centric means you recognise this and behave accordingly. If your demeanour is good, you're warm and welcoming, customers will soon open up to you if they're looking for anything more than this and that's why the simple courtesies are so important because they pave the way for the customer to engage with you when it suits them. Missing simple courtesies puts you on the back foot from the very start.

Some of you will argue that your business or place of work just doesn't warrant that level of engagement. Maybe you're a newsagent, a pound shop or a kiosk where people don't generally spend more than a fiver at any one time. Sure, I see your point but how many of these people are in your businesses every day or at least more than once a week? You know I am willing to bet that there are those of you who work in or own these types of business that will recognise many of your frequent customers and remember the brand of cigarette they buy or which daily newspaper they generally take. Those of you that are really switched on will have already asked these customers if they want their paper reserved for them or even delivered to their door. So there really is no argument here, being customer centric is a key behaviour of all professional hosts regardless of the level of environment they work in.

Small and local businesses normally pick this up quite quickly, which is why they tend to do so much better than the national companies in the customer service stakes. Big companies mistakenly believe that their business structure stops them from being customer centric and they look for other ways to engage with their customers. Many businesses operate central customer service teams to manage customer feedback and complaints, but this isn't being customer centric at all, it's a structure designed to suit the needs of their business not the needs of their customers. Some also mistakenly believe that they are being customer centric by pro-actively surveying their customers – perhaps the most common of which has the very promising title of 'Customer Satisfaction Index' but by and large are way off the mark. I explain why this is in the next chapter.

For now I'm just going to finish this chapter by reminding you of the difference between being customer centric (which is what we should all aim for) and being business centric, which is what most larger companies are. My experience with Wessex Water was one where the importance of internal processes outweighed the importance of customer needs. When this occurs you have a business that is business centric, inwardly focusing, where the customer is required to adhere to company policy in order to progress.

On a smaller scale I can cite the example of a local estate agents business that decided it wouldn't open at weekends because it suited the owner and the staff otherwise. Well sorry guys, but some of us are working flat out during the week and only have the weekend to deal with house-hunting. It might suit you not to work the weekends but potential buyers won't be best pleased. In a tough downward market you will be one of the first businesses to fail.

And finally, the title of most 'business centric company' I have ever come across must surely go to a lovely little café out by the lakes to the south of Bristol whose policy was to close for lunch! What the…?!

Customer surveys – Pretending to be interested

So many businesses delude themselves that they are interested in their customers because they regularly survey them to find out what they think. Phooey – that's an absolute crock.

Customer surveys in the main are business centric, that is to say that the information they gather is for the benefit of the business not for the customer. How do we know this? Well for starters they are all about the business.

Well I say how come I have to answer your questions? How come I have to provide you with information you want? What about what I want to say? Where is there room in this questionnaire for what I want to say? And how come whenever I fill in these things you don't even want to know my name? And how come if I do manage to scribble a note somewhere in the margin I never get to hear back from you?

Next, tick box questionnaires by their very nature use 'closed field' questions. A 'closed field' question is one that limits the response to a finite selection provided for you, for example…

*   Which daily newspapers do your read?

    The Sun ☐   The Mirror ☐   The Mail ☐   The Observer ☐

This question is closed field because you are only able to select a response from the four answers provided for you. 'open field' questions are often presented in the same way but offer no limitations to the response so that we would see the following…

*   Which daily newspapers do your read?

    The Independent
    The Guardian

It's easy to see in these examples the critical difference between open and closed field questions. To me it's obvious that any business that uses closed field questions is doing so because they want to restrict my responses.

Let's remember, customers aren't stupid. We all know that completing customer surveys gives us no direct benefit. That's why companies have to bribe us with vouchers, prize draws and holiday offers. They need to entice us to complete their surveys, because otherwise we just wouldn't be bothered – why should we be?

Don't get me wrong, I'm not saying that there is no place for surveys of this sort – without question they serve a purpose, they provide good quality statistical information that businesses can use to evaluate their products and services, and form part of a broader marketing research function. But they shouldn't be confused with customer feedback, which is a completely different kettle of fish. One is about what the business wants to know, the other is about what the customer wants to tell you. Which do you think has the greater positive impact on the customer experience?

Let me try to elaborate on the differences. I have seen for myself the frustrations customers have when they are presented with these closed field surveys. Often these poor customers have had such an awful experience with a particular business or service that they feel compelled to write down their anguish wherever they can find space on the questionnaire. Ignoring all the tick boxes and scribbling frantically in the margins or wherever white space presents itself. Well folks if that's you, I've got some bad news for you – you might as well have not bothered.

In fact, writing anything outside of those tick boxes is a complete waste of time! You see businesses that use these tick box questionnaires don't read them when they get them back. In fact they don't get anywhere near them because on the whole when you return your questionnaire it ends up at a completely different data processing company. This company is a high volume data specialist that stacks your completed questionnaire, along with several thousand others, on to a special OCR machine that is programmed to log each box ticked and programmed to reject any spoiled questionnaires (by the way, if you've taken the time to write anything on the questionnaire you have in fact spoiled it).

So you see any response outside the tick boxes this questionnaire has set out for you are not wanted, in fact they're rejected or ignored – but why? Why after you have taken so much trouble to write your comments in the 2cm of space in the left hand column of page two should they just reject it without even taking the time to read what you felt was so important to say? It's because they are making the process of customer feedback suit the company, not the customer.

It doesn't have to be this way.

Customer feedback and closed field surveys can actually work very well together if you apply a few key rules. Firstly, understand that what the customer wants to tell you is more important to them than what you want to know. So start by letting them express themselves as much and as far as they would like. Customers will feel much better about their relationship with you if you show them that their thoughts and opinions have the highest level of importance. Once you have allowed your customers to express themselves you can ask them to help you with the information you want to know.

So why do businesses get lost in doing tick box surveys rather than asking for specific responses? Well, in general, it's the marketing department that takes responsibility for the creation of these survey questionnaires. Even in very large companies there are likely to be only four or five individuals at the most tasked with managing the customer responses. Such a small team is incapable of dealing with thousands upon thousands of individual customer feedback responses, so they generalise. They get everybody to complete the same series of questions and group all the responses together in to a percentage statistic – easy to manage, easy to work with. The purpose of gathering this information isn't to deliver a great customer experience, it is number chasing – the purpose of gathering statistical information.

In my business we carried out such an exercise with tick boxes on behalf of a client with an internationally recognised brand. I advised them that we had a large number of questionnaires returned with handwritten comments and notes – I was told to put them in the bin because the company had no internal structure to deal with them! Client confidentiality prohibits me from telling you who they are and in any case we are working hard with this particular client to get their act together.

The fact is that customer surveys of this type serve a limited purpose and that doesn't include customer satisfaction. They're OK, I guess, if you're looking for broad data pictures but even then I think they are lacking, I'll explain why.

A few years ago, I took the opportunity to grab a quick half-term break with the wife and kids, and set off to Cyprus for a week. It was supposedly a 4 star hotel and on the whole it was OK. After all we were only going to be there for a week. On the return flight, we got the mandatory 'How was your holiday' questionnaire and, being a bit of a questionnaire freak, I decided I would complete it to see what it was all about.

As I expected it was nothing more than a series of questions asking me for information that the tour company wanted to know about. I remember in particular a collection of questions that were all about the transfer from the airport to the hotel. Well to tell you the truth I hadn't given the transfer much thought – I mean we were only on the coach for maybe 20 minutes and there really wasn't much to say but I guess if you're asking:

- The driver looked like he fell out of a bush
- So did his cigarette
- The air-con could have been a little cooler
- The coach was a little dusty
- The seats were a little raggedy
- It could have done with a quick Dyson.

Thing is, it didn't really matter all that much to me. But what if all the other passengers on that same flight said the same things and it didn't really matter that much to them either? Well, one might think that the tour company would look at these responses and think they had a calamity on their hands! They might insist to the coach operator that he had his air-con serviced every three months and that his drivers all wear uniforms, and that the coaches are cleaned inside and out before each customer pick up. They may well put in place far reaching policies to improve the whole process of transfers to and from the airport, incur significant additional cost and it would make no difference whatsoever to their customers, who weren't really bothered in the first place. It is one thing asking for information but if you don't measure the importance of that information how can you possibly use it to make effective judgements?

Furthermore, tick box questionnaires confine customer answers only to the options listed. If, using my tick box questionnaire, I were to ask you if you preferred HP baked beans or Branston baked beans, you would need to give me one answer or another – let's say you indicated you preferred Branston baked beans to HP. So if you're Mr Branston you're feeling a bit chuffed right now, after all you said you preferred to buy his baked beans didn't you? Well no, you didn't.

What you said was that you preferred Branston's baked beans to HP baked beans – that's because you think HP beans really suck and anything has to be better than them. The fact is you haven't even tried Branston's baked beans you always buy Heinz, but we didn't ask you that did we?

So tick box questionnaires only ever offer the customer a 'best fit' option. Many marketing companies recognise this and try to drill down with more specific questions in order to define a customer's preferences in more granular detail. With closed field tick boxes if you want to gauge where a customer is as accurately as you can you have to provide them with as many response options as is available. For example, earlier on we asked the question: "Which daily newspaper do you read?" To get as accurate data as possible to this question we would need to list all ten main national publications that are available (Mail, Mirror, Sun, Guardian, Independent, Times, Telegraph, Express, Star and Financial Times), each with their own tick box.

But still, even though we have gone to great lengths to offer the biggest choice of newspapers tick boxes possible we might still get it wrong if the customer actually reads the Evening Standard as their daily paper.

Let's look at it from a baked beans perspective again. In order to get as accurate data as possible I really need to list as many baked bean brands as possible. Do you have any idea how many different brands of baked beans there are out there if you include things like supermarket own brands? But let's just say that we've put together a pretty comprehensive list of Baked Bean Brands and we've managed to persuade our customer to look at them all to choose their favourite – and let's just say that luckily our list of baked bean brands actually includes their favourite.

OK now I want to know why it's their favourite and here's where it gets tricky! Was it the tomato sauce? Was it the sweetness of the sauce? Was it the colour of the sauce? The thickness? Was it the beans? Was it the number of beans in the can? The size of the beans? Was it the easy open lid? The size of the can? And so on, and on, and on…

In fact to get the level of detail I need from a tick box questionnaire I have to include hundreds or boxes. Any of you that have visited Center Parcs in days of old and had been given one of their questionnaires will know exactly what I mean (although it is now all online).

Center Parcs questionnaire was four pages of A4 smashed full of so many little tick boxes that you needed a magnifying glass to see them. They had completely lost the plot with this document and were trying to get granular detail not just on Center Parcs as a whole but also on each catering establishment and for each activity centre. Even though I'm a questionnaire freak I didn't think I had enough life to complete this one! No doubt they will tell you that loads of their visitors complete the questionnaire and that they get very meaningful and useful information from them – but you can bet your boots they don't get the important stuff.

The stuff like the fact that I don't do Center Parcs anymore because it keeps building more and more accommodation on the site without increasing the facilities. You can't get in the pool and you can't get a table to eat – and its too expensive for the mediocre service that is has become. Bet I'm not the only one who's noticed?

Don't get me wrong, I don't have an axe to grind with Center Parcs, I just won't go their much anymore. They probably haven't noticed. They send me emails every week but they never ask why I haven't visited them for a few years when I was such a regular visitor – I wonder why?

So you can see, hundreds of tick boxes might be acceptable to you if you're the marketing department of a large company but it's certainly not acceptable to your customers. Why? Because you're excessive questions illustrate your demand for information but don't show any interest in my personal experiences.

Some companies try and be clever by adding a little line space at the end of their questionnaire or perhaps a small empty box somewhere for the customer to add a comment. But the mere fact that this space, solely for the use of the customer, is so small and insignificant shows that the business isn't really that interested and probably doesn't want you to say anything.

My holiday questionnaire is testament to that fact, I had the normal collections of tick box questions asking me to rate the hotel and the rep and did I take this excursion and that excursion and how did I rate each of them – and so it went on for two or three pages when finally I got to a single line on the back of the questionnaire with the title 'Customer Comment'. Wow, that's a bit impersonal, how about something like 'your thoughts' or 'is there anything you would like to tell us?' 'Customer Comment' is just a bit curt.

And come on!
One line?
Just one line?

I mean I've told you everything you wanted to know and now you give me just one line to say what I want to say? I want to tell you that the walls in our room were paper thin – and that the guy in the room next door had prostate trouble because every time he got up in the middle of the night (and there were lots of them) we could hear him peeing.

I want to tell you that when we asked to be moved we wish we hadn't because even though the grumpy manager gave us another room it was right at the front of the building and that every morning at 4.30am the bottle recycling bin would be emptied, which woke us up and woke up the dog outside who then proceeded to bark for the next two hours until the sun came up or someone kicked it. That's what I want to tell you! But how the hell can I tell you this on just one line??!

And so for me, the most telling factor about these questionnaires is that all of the content is all about what the company wants to know – and the bit for me, the customer bit is rarely offered. Isn't that the clearest indication of all on my importance and value to them as a customer?

Many upbeat, forward thinking businesses are aware that tick boxes aren't the way to go when it comes to customer service and more importantly they recognise that unless you measure the importance of the response you can get a skewed result. Their answer to this is to ask much more considered questions and look to measure importance through a progressive scale. These are the ones you will recognise that ask you the extent to which you agree with a statement – you know the ones that say are you:

- Dissatisfied
- A little dissatisfied
- Neither satisfied nor dissatisfied

- A little satisfied
- Very satisfied

Mmmmm, something not quite right here. Surely you're either satisfied or you're not? I mean it's a little bit like being dead, you're either dead or you're not, you can't be a little bit dead and neither can you be a little bit satisfied. It's either all good in which case you're satisfied or something (no matter how small) is not right, in which case you're not satisfied – its one or the other, right? So what's this all about? Do companies really look at their statistics and say 32% of our customers were a bit satisfied? You bet your life they do!

You see they get tangled up in the 'satisfaction' bit of their 'Customer Satisfaction Survey' and miss the point completely that it should in fact be the 'Customer Experience Survey'. It's the overall experience that counts, little dissatisfactions here or there are quite normal but irrelevant when looking at the whole picture. Just like my transfer from the airport to the hotel, I guess I wasn't satisfied with it, but do you know what on the whole it didn't matter because the holiday overall was great. And this gets me to the point that really customer surveys need to be far more customer focused. Here's how I think a truly customer centric questionnaire should go:

1. Please tell us your thoughts about your experience with us?

That's it, that's all – this is the one true customer centric questionnaire. It is totally customer facing, it allows the customer to set the agenda and tell us what is important to them as an individual customer. You can be sure that whatever response you get it will be important, customers won't waste their time talking about trivialities or things that really don't matter all that much to them.

Notice, in my questionnaire of one question that I didn't ask them for their name, that's not because I'm not interested, it's because I already know their name. They're my customer and it's my business to know all about them. I know what they bought from me and when, how many times they've had it serviced, when and what for. I know if they're happy with my business and what things they like best about us and what things they would like us to work on and because I know all this my customer will never buy from anyone else – they love us!

So, a customer feedback questionnaire should only be one question long and it should be open so that the customer can give feedback whenever they want to and not just when the business sends out a questionnaire. In a practical world only one question might be spot on for the customer but it's likely to be completely unworkable for many businesses, even the ones that are really good at being customer focused. Adding one or two other carefully crafted questions can help businesses manage the customer responses without imposing too much on the customer – and in general I believe that customers expect to answer a few questions because of this. However, in my opinion there is never any reason for the number of questions on a feedback questionnaire to reach double figures.

Thing is my one question is completely unpredictable. When we ask this question we can never be sure what sort of response we will get. Will it be a compliment or a complaint? Will it require action or is it just for our information? In short, each individual response will need to be individually digested. It will need to be read in its entirety regardless of whether its 100 words or 10,000 words. The reader will need to be on the lookout for specific comments, demands and requests.

Now you're probably thinking that that's a lot of work right there. You're probably thinking about how many customers you have and if just 10% of them make a comment how many staff you are going to need to sit there and read all that verbatim? It's a big task for sure, but it's achievable in most cases as you will see in a moment.

Some of you may already be ahead of the game, especially the more technically proficient ones. You already know that there are software companies out there developing systems especially designed for reading and deciphering consumer feedback.

Don't be fooled that there are artificially intelligent software programmes out there that can do this for you – at the time or writing this the technology just isn't there yet. Language is constantly shifting and is full of subtleties, for example 'bad' is good and 'wicked' is better – if I explain how disappointed I am in the service I have received and finish my response along the lines "you can rest assured that all my friends will get to hear about just how good your service was" you would draw the conclusion that I am using sarcasm to heighten my point. You are able to make this assessment because you have understood the comment in the context of the overall negative response given, whereas the various software analysis tools that are currently available will simply see 'how good your service was' and make the wrong judgement.

Those of you that are considering using such tools should be cautious to the extent to which you are using them and bear in mind that they put you back in the process of generalising customer responses, in the same way that tick boxes do, moving you away from being customer centric. The fact that so many reputable businesses have even considered such software shows that they know how to ask the right questions but don't know what to do with the answers. The solution is relatively simple but requires a complete change of culture.

A couple of years ago, I was invited to help one of the world's leading brands of sports car, Porsche, develop a system, a process if you will, to help them get closer to their customers. Porsche's reputation for building cars was unrivalled and as a business it was the most profitable car manufacturer in the world. Unfortunately, the reputation of the Porsche dealership did not match up to the reputation of the car and this disparity was a key driver for change.

By the time we got involved Porsche had already made significant positive changes to its business model, of which one of the largest undertakings was the re-branding of its dealership network. Up until then, most dealerships were independent businesses trading in their own right and in their own name. Porsche were able to negotiate an agreement with its dealership network that would see them drop their individual identity to be replaced with a common unilateral brand that was Porsche. The thinking was that the Porsche customer should be able to take their car to any Porsche dealership for any matter and need not be concerned whether or not they were individual companies with their own profit and loss accounts. Quite right so, if I buy a pair of trousers from Marks & Spencer I can take them back to any of their stores, not just the store from which I purchased them.

This was very much a positive step but it needed to be supported with a strong customer engagement programme that took a genuine interest in the customer and their experience with Porsche. At that time, like most other motor manufacturers, Porsche had a rigid customer satisfaction survey that they used with their customers. Being a premium brand Porsche thought the right approach would be to contact their customers directly by telephone, rather than send them all a faceless tick box questionnaire – nice sentiment. Sadly 150 questions on a tick box questionnaire is one thing but being faced with a telephone survey of the same size is daunting for both the customer and the surveyor if not extremely off putting.

And this in fact was the position that Porsche found themselves in. At that time I was introduced to a super (and pleasantly eccentric) customer experience consultant who had quickly identified the flaws in this approach and quite rightly pointed out that the customer survey itself should be a positive experience, which it was clearly not. He had already embarked on a programme of research with an internal Porsche working group, which resulted in a number of recommendations on how they should engage their customers through a customer satisfaction survey. He identified the need to move away from prescribed answers of the sort you would find on tick box questionnaires, instead moving to more open questions that let the customer set the agenda, questions like:

- What was the experience about?
- Was the experience mainly positive or mainly negative?
- Why do you feel this way?
- How would you rate the experience?
- How can we improve?

The problem was that this move towards more customer centric processes was being driven internally through Porsche's marketing department who simply did not have the head count to manage thousands of individual customer responses. And it was this conundrum that eventually got he and I talking.

To me it was relatively obvious. Customers were in the main communicating their experiences of dealing with Porsche at local dealership level. After all it was here where the customer would have purchased their vehicle and here where they would have it serviced. It seemed clear to me that the principal relationship between Porsche and its customers lay at the dealership, not through the marketing or customer service department.

Dealership staff would know and recognise the customer, they would know how many cars the customer owned and had ever bought from them. They would know if the customer was a proverbial pain in the butt or easy to please with a little TLC. They would know when he last had his car serviced and how much it cost him. They would probably even know if he liked to play golf and what his handicap was. In fact they would know just about everything there was available to know about this customer and would therefore be best placed to deal with any matter that might arise from a customer satisfaction survey.

It wasn't necessary for Porsche at head office to deal with individual queries. In fact they couldn't possibly expect to deal with customer issues more effectively than the dealer, how could they? They had no experience of the circumstances at hand, they would have only limited notes as were available and they would be building their experience of the customer from scratch. It seemed only logical that it was the dealer that should take responsibility for managing customer responses.

Armed with this knowledge we devised and built a software system called 'Your Impressions™' that was able to deliver individual customer satisfaction survey responses directly to the relevant dealership in such a way that the customer was able to set the agenda as to what it was they wanted to say. Dealers were provided with a set of simple tools that helped them monitor responses as well as address any specific concerns raised within minutes of receiving them. The system still retained essential reporting that let the marketing team and head office measure key areas of their business and react to poor performances. Yet to all intents and purposes it was the closest thing, in all the entire motor industry, to a customer centric survey.

The effect of the new Your Impressions™ system was astounding. Dealerships and customers alike warmed to it immediately. Its real time functionality often meant that hitherto unknown 'problems' were often resolved in a matter of minutes. Dealers liked it because it, more often than not, made them aware of problems that would never have come to light and customers liked it because the system responded to their requirements allowing them to say what they wanted, when they wanted. In a year the Porsche satisfaction survey went from 12th place to 2nd overall in the Sewells dealer survey and progress was good.

But there's nothing here that I haven't mentioned before, what we were able to achieve with Porsche was a system that put ownership of the customer and their feedback squarely at dealer level. As I have said before it is the degree of ownership that ultimately determines the degree of customer service but it's not all plain sailing. Having opened the flood gates to customer feedback many Porsche dealers found themselves without the necessary skills to manage responses and often compounded difficult situations by inept and inappropriate action. Still, Porsche were revolutionary in their approach to customer service and I have no doubt that they will continue to improve their approach.

But not every car manufacturer is as forward thinking as Porsche. I recently bought a FIAT 500 convertible from a local dealer Wessex Garages (who incidentally are probably one of the most forward thinking car dealerships in the UK when it comes to putting the customer first – they should be, they're one of my local flagship clients).

Now I love this car to bits – I love it because it's a throw back to my youth when my father owned one of the original 500s. I love it because for the first time in as long as I can remember I no longer struggle to park – I love it because FIAT have achieved marvellous things with their styling and engineering and I love it because for all intents and purposes this is a large executive saloon in a small city car – get one, you'll love it too!

But despite the fabulous service I received from Wessex Garages I couldn't wait for the telephone call from FIAT so that I could tell them all about my fabulous car and how much I loved it, except the call never came.

Now not being one to be outdone, I decided I would call FIAT myself and find out why they hadn't called me to see if everything was OK? It turns out the FIAT (and they're not alone in this by the way) don't call every customer that buys one of their cars – in fact they only call a small sample of customers, a few from each of their dealers.

I have to say I was really disappointed in this – to me FIAT had done wondrous things with their cars, which up to only a few short years ago were (I have to be honest) rubbish. But they had reinvented themselves and their cars were now really rather good and I had the impression that the rest of their business would be really rather good as well. But sadly they weren't as interested in me as I was in them, they never took the time to ask me about my experience or how I felt about my car and I have to say that left me feeling as if my business wasn't particularly valued. Turns out I wasn't the only one to feel this way.

In my attempts to contact FIAT about this I Googled 'FIAT Head Office Number' and what I found was several pages of forums where disgruntled FIAT owners had taken the opportunity to air their grievances in public. Now this wasn't good, I mean there were pages and pages of this stuff all of which were taking great big pot shots at FIAT and their cars. It occurred to me that this was probably as a direct result of FIAT's customer survey policy (that only engages such a small percentage of their customers).

It's pretty clear, that if you only ask a sample of your customer base how they feel about their experience with you then you demonstrate that your survey is carried out solely for the benefit of the business. After all, how could you possibly identify and resolve any customer problems or queries if you don't speak to every customer in the first place? In truth FIAT is showing that they're not interested in the customer, only in collating statistics to monitor the performance of their dealer network – this is a process I call number chasing, the pursuit of a benchmark score from customers for purposes other than addressing specific issues raised.

Not surprising then that disillusioned customers with no way of communicating their issues with FIAT resort to public forums to, at the very least, vent their spleen and release a little pent up frustration. For me the solution is particularly simple – FIAT need to change their approach and show a little interest in their customers. They should allow anyone that buys one of their cars the opportunity to engage with them to establish how good the experience was and to put right things that have gone wrong.

Here's a good quote that sums this up:

"Customers don't expect you to be perfect. They do expect you to fix things when they go wrong." Donald Porter V.P., British Airways

And if FIAT took this approach they would achieve two things almost overnight, they would practically eradicate any negative publicity on public forums (after all customers would be able to address their issues directly with FIAT). And secondly and most importantly, they would show their customers that they're interested in them and that they value them – this is the 'Golden Rule' the first and most important step towards building customer loyalty and positive advocacy.

Asking customers what they think about their experience with you is not just important, it's essential! It's essential because it's the only way to find out what your customers are telling everybody else about you. It's essential because a well constructed, customer centric feedback questionnaire will determine whether or not consumer word–of–mouth is working for you or against you and believe it or not it is word–of–mouth that will determine whether your business succeeds or fails.

Some final points about online public forums, which shows why they are so dangerous and should be avoided at all costs. Firstly, they are totally one-sided and in nearly all cases illustrate only the customers' point of view – businesses don't generally even have the opportunity to comment, even if it's just to say sorry. Secondly, they are only a snap shot in time and illustrate the customer's perception at the time of writing – they make no provision at all for any subsequent contact with the company or resolution thereafter and so are in most cases not remotely a true reflection of the circumstances to date. Those individuals posting negative comments and opinions on forums are unlikely to post amendments or updates – so there's no telling whether or not the offending company has actually dealt with the situation in an very positive manner. You can tell this if you take the time to see when the comment was posted – some of them are years old and never get taken down!

And just to be clear – closed field, tick box research surveys are a much needed business tool and serve a valuable purpose, but don't confuse them with experience or feedback surveys. One is about what you want to know, the other is about what the customer wants to tell you and it's the latter that provides all the information you will ever need to build strong and loyal customer relationships.

Now here's the clever bit! Our system Your Impressions™ combines these two aspects leading with what the customer wants to say before asking what the business wants to know. The business gets all the metrics it needs while strengthening the relationship it has with its customers and building its reputation.

Just to put some numbers on this, we did our own research and discovered that 79% of customers that engaged with a company feedback survey had specific comments and opinions of their own that they wanted to make. If that's not an indication of the importance of 'what the customer wants to say', I don't know what is.

Incidentally, in our research over 96% or respondents that were given the opportunity to vocalise their own thoughts and opinions then went on to complete the full tick box survey. This is because asking them about their opinions shows that you are interested in them, it engages them in the process of giving comment and while in that mind set they are much more include to provide further information that you specifically want.

One final point, if your customers are going to go to the trouble of giving you their feedback, then it's essential that you react to it as soon as possible. A good software system like Your Impressions™ can help you with that.

Dealing with feedback

I debated whether or not I should write any content on managing feedback in this book and figured that if we looked at how to capture feedback then it would be remiss of me not to give you a few pointers on how to manage it.

The first and most important thing to consider when managing feedback is that it's not necessarily a reflection of actual circumstances, here's a great quote for you from Mark Perrault at Rally Stores:

"If the shopper feels like it was poor service, then it was poor service. We are in the customer perception business."

I like this quote because it perfectly illustrates my point. When we get feedback from customers we are actually getting an opinion, a viewpoint. And that viewpoint may have only a passing resemblance to your perception of the very same experience.

The point Mark makes is that we can all forget about what we think happened, that doesn't matter. What matters is what the customer thought happened and it is their perception that we have to address and manage. So don't be surprised if you get customer feedback that you think is unwarranted or unfair, concern yourself more with how and why your customer got to feel that way in the first place.

First off, it's absolutely essential that you acknowledge all feedback you receive, good and bad. This shows the customer that you have taken the time to sit and digest their comments, which in turn shows that you are interested in them and therefore, by default, value them and their business – absolutely essential for building affinity.

Now, if you're dealing with negative feedback you must react to it straightaway if not sooner. Most people do not expect a reaction to feedback, so imagine how impressed they will be if within moments of giving you their opinions they get a response. It shows that you and your team are on the ball and that your customers' opinions are important to you. Essential in building a loyal customer base and more importantly turning a negative experience into a positive one.

If you are dealing with written feedback there are a few things you need to understand, particularly with negative feedback.

When a customer interacts with your business they have a certain expectation on how that interaction will go, as we have already explored in this book. When circumstances are worse than the expectation the customer is in the throes of enduring a bad experience. This has the negative effect of creating hypersensitivity, a state of mind where the customer becomes increasingly aware of negative aspects of your products and service. Things that would not normally have been of concern (or even noticed) are now serving only to compound the negative experience.

Quite often this is reflected in the feedback you get in the form of a long diatribe that lists out extensive failures in your business and your business process. Much of this could be considered 'nit picking' and some may even be pure conjecture, assumptions of failure on your part. I'm going to illustrate this by sharing with you some actual customer feedback I found on the internet about a customer that had visited a local garage. Bear with me, it goes on a bit but is a great example of how customers become hypersensitive:

"I enquired about a service for my car over a month ago and to chase the garage up about an outstanding warranty repair. I was pleased with the competitive quote I was given. I asked for a courtesy car and had to argue why I shouldn't have to pay for it when the visit was including a warranty repair, this was resolved easily in the end.

"I dropped the car off on Monday morning, no problem and was informed at 5pm that my car was ready, we agreed due to the time a morning pick up was fine. Upon collecting the car at 8.30am on the 12th, I paid the lady and asked whether the warranty book in the car had been stamped, which I had left on the passenger side in clear sight, I was assured it was done.

"In the evening when I had time to examine the documents and breakdown of the service, the following problems were found:

1. The warranty book had NOT been stamped
2. The 'service due' mileage on the car's computer had not been re-set (18,000 miles)
3. The grade of oil used was incorrect and no engine flush had been performed.

"I asked for a competitive service price not an incorrect service. The car is designed for fully synthetic oil and semi–synthetic oil was put in it. Having a PhD in chemistry I know the difference and I know this change is not good for the car. I feel this is very bad practice, giving a deceptionally cheap service with sub–standard parts.

"Further to this the car had never leaked a drop up until the service on Monday the 11th. I have examined the car and it seems like the oil filter and sump plug are incorrectly tightened AND/OR the person performing the service spilt oil everywhere and did not clean it up of the sump guard and it has now run off while on a slight slope on the drive."

It's quite clear here that a number of failings on the part of the workshop have brought into question the competency of their service. A couple of the specific examples the customer gives cannot be questioned, the service book wasn't stamped and the 'next service' date not reset on the cars computer.

What's really interesting is where the customer goes from there, particularly a number of assumptions that are nothing but pure conjecture:

"... I just arrived home to notice a large puddle of oil on the floor of my drive."

The assumption is that the workshop are at fault and I suppose that would be a natural assumption, it would be a bit of a coincidence if otherwise. Secondly, what constitutes a "large puddle?" I would expect that in fact this oil spillage was relatively minor but that the customer's state of hypersensitivity has exacerbated their perception of the problem.

"I have examined the car and it seems like the oil filter and sump plug are incorrectly tightened..."

OK, so how does this customer know that the sump plug is incorrectly tightened? Is it possible that this customer has jacked up their car and using the appropriate tools checked to see if the sump plug was correctly fitted? Of course not, it's pure conjecture, which supported by the very next statement:

"AND/OR the person performing the service spilt oil everywhere and did not clean it up of the sump guard and it has now run off while on a slight slope on the drive."

So maybe it has nothing at all to do with the sump plug and is due to poor practice on the part of the service engineer – or maybe it's both!!

The fact is that based on their experience with the workshop so far this customer has made a series of assumptions that don't necessarily have any bearing on the facts.

But guess what, that doesn't matter, because once we get past the stuff that is conjecture we can see that there are underlying incompetencies that caused them to be hypertensive in the first place. Key for you is to cut through the unnecessary comment and look for the underlying causes and deal with those.

Don't get hung up arguing the toss about whether or not the sump plug was correctly tightened, deal with the tangibles:

1. The warranty book had NOT been stamped
2. The 'service due' mileage on the car's computer had not been re-set (18,000 miles).

This is the crux of what went wrong and sadly in this instance I suspect that had these two items been properly attended to in the first place the customer would have perceived a completely different experience.

The wonderful thing about written feedback of this type is that it's the perfect steer for what you need to do to put things right. Customers will list out their concerns and it's this very same list that you can work from in order to put things right. It really couldn't be easier.

So, we know that feedback is perception and that customers can perceive all sorts of things some of which have no real bearing at all. We know that we have to dig deep to get to the real nuts and bolts of the issue and that this in turn will lead us on the correct course to put things right.

There's much more later on in this book on how to manage customers in difficult situations but getting a good understanding on how to deal with feedback is the first step in putting things right and turning a negative experience into a loyal customer.

Word–of–mouth – The measurement of Buzz

Traditional forms of media normally associated with advertising are losing their effectiveness on the general public. People are sharper than they have ever been and see straight through hyped up media messages. Cleverly constructed adverts designed to create a purchase desire are being met with scepticism and in some cases distain. How can such advertising offer unbiased messages when they are bought and paid for by the company selling its wares? Well the answer is that they can't and recognising this many companies are resorting to a strategy that promotes brand recognition rather than a call to action.

Who could forget the fantastic Cadbury's advert that featured the gorilla playing drums to the classic Phil Collins track 'In the air tonight?' Sorry, run that passed me again, what the hell did that advert have to do with chocolate? Where was the message compelling me to go out and buy 40 chocolate bars that very moment?

It was a superbly considered advert that was about promoting brand awareness for Cadbury. It didn't mention a single one of their specific confectionery products but it was then most talked about advert of its time.

So how do consumers choose which product to buy when they place such marginal reliance on the media messages they are constantly being bombarded with? Well, there's no doubt that adverts like the Cadbury's gorilla build brand recognition, which in turn builds consumer trust and puts you at least on the list when it comes to buying chocolate. Outside of this, consumers more and more seek word–of–mouth recommendations to help them decide their purchase decisions and it's clear why.

Word–of–mouth is free. It is a borrowed experience that has nothing to sell other than itself. Let's be clear, it is not unbiased, in fact the opposite is true – enthusiastic exponents of word or mouth advice will go to great lengths to encourage or discourage you from buying a particular product or using a particular service. But this enthusiasm is built on genuine experience and is therefore from a reputable source that can be trusted. People place great credence on word–of–mouth feedback. Endorsing a product, a company or brand carries with it a degree of risk in the event that recommendations fall short of expectation. Therefore people are unlikely to give their endorsement unless they can be reasonably certain that the service or product they are recommending will deliver according to their own experience. This means that word-of-mouth endorsements carry significant weight when it comes to making purchase decisions.

This fact is well-known and a collaboration in the USA between Satmetrix, Bain & Co. and Fred Reichheld used this premise as the basis for research into customer loyalty. Their research determined that customer questionnaires did little to assess the level of loyalty customers felt towards a particular brand or product and through a process of evaluation they determined that all that was required to establish this was one, well constructed question that became known as 'the ultimate question'. I'm pretty sure that it's a question that you will recognise and have probably even answered yourself:

"On a scale of 0 to 10, where 10 is definitely, how likely are you to recommend this product/company/brand to your friends, family and colleagues?"

Knowing that consumers were unlikely to score highly if they felt there was some chance that the product or service would not come up to scratch the team were able to separate respondents into 3 key loyalty groups against the score they provided.

Score 0 to 6 – Detractors
Score 7 to 8 – Neutrals
Score 9 to10 – Promoters

Now let's examine each of these in a little more detail:

Detractors

This is the largest of these groups if we consider it by range of score (0 to 6), and the term detractors describes perfectly customers who are exactly that. People that for whatever reason (usually as a result of a bad service experience) actively sought to discourage their friends and colleagues from using a particular company or brand. They were particularly sensitive to price and very hard to please. They were likely to be hypersensitive noticing every defect and fault, even very minor issues become blown out of all proportion as the customer spirals downward into an increasingly negative experience and relationship.

Each of us will have experienced bad service at some point and this will have shaped the way we think about the company and our attitude towards them. I'm going to quote you some statistics from The Customer Experience Report of 2006, which are totally relevant even to this day. The report examined customer attitudes towards bad service and the impact it had on their affinity with the company. Perhaps the most astonishing figure to come out of this report was that respondents said that 25% of all their experiences as customers were negative! Can you imagine that, a quarter, one in four customer experiences was a bad one!

This sets the scale of the problem when it comes to negative experiences and it's hard to imagine that any of us could go a day without some form of bad service. But in some ways the sheer scale of the problem also exacerbates it. Bad service has become part of everyday life and we accept it just as we would traffic jams, wet summers or any other common place occurrence. I mean, of all of us, who truly expects to get good quality service wherever we go, I bet not many. Sure, you'll expect to get top draw service from the swanky restaurant in the city centre, but do you have any expectation of decent service say from a national electronics retailer or motor dealership or fast food chain? I have to say that sadly I don't.

This might also shed a little light on the next statistic to emerge from the report that 65% of respondents moved their business elsewhere after a bad service experience. Now, I had to think about this one a little – sad to say I expect pretty poor service on the whole and if I went moving my business elsewhere every time I had a bad service experience I would be constantly looking for new retailers and suppliers.

Having said that if I had a really bad experience, I mean of the sort of proportions I have illustrated in this book time and time again I would indeed have moved my business elsewhere, never to return. Perhaps this is why 38% of respondents that moved their business elsewhere following a bad service experience stated that the organisation would have to prove that it valued their custom for them to return.

We take it personally – and so we should!

Let's not forget that we are parting with hard earned cash, cash that contributes to the salaries and therefore livelihoods of those individuals that have been less than acceptable in serving us (and I may well be referring to some of you reading this book). It's quite natural then to be somewhat peeved and to take it as a personal rebuke. This would explain why 27% of all respondents indicated that once their business was lost it was lost forever! I can vouch for that personally.

Having moved into my new home more than a decade ago, I proceeded to undertake a lot of structural work that saw me take a building that had been previously split into two and restore it to its original single dwelling status.

Being two dwellings when I bought it, the house came with two gas meters, nothing unusual about that I thought at the time. One was disconnected and the other used as the sole meter for supply to the property – all under the watchful eye of British Gas, my supplier at the time.

You can imagine my surprise when some three months later I received a quarterly bill, which included a rental charge for a gas meter that hadn't even been in operation. Of course I contacted British Gas to ask them why this was the case and they advised me that as I had the meter a rental was due regardless of whether or not I had used it. On the face of it I guess that's probably right, but the problem here is that British Gas failed to act in the customers best interests.

They clearly knew that one of the meters had been disconnected – at the very least by the lack of any gas usage, yet they chose to continue to allow me to incur charges without even checking with me to ensure that this was acceptable.

You might argue as did they that the meter was under agreement and that it was my responsibility to ensure that I cancelled the agreement and had the meter removed and perhaps contractually that is so. However from a customer service view point that attitude sucks. I gave British Gas every opportunity to address the situation and asked them to remove the meter and credit back the rental charges for the unused meter but they refused and so I voted with my feet and moved my business elsewhere.

That was well more than 10 years ago and despite a number of opportunities to move back to British Gas to take advantage of more competitive energy prices I have not – and will not! In fact for as long as I live and breathe I won't use British Gas on principal, not in any capacity.

I expect that there are a few of you out there suggesting that I am cutting my nose off to spite my face and that British Gas probably don't give two hoots about me in any case and that maybe so – but let's not forget the power of word-of-mouth advocacy. I have spoken with many people since this incident and told them of my disdain for British Gas and during that time I am positive that one or two will have thought twice about buying from British Gas. And of course think about the long term loss of revenue they would have gained from me for the sake of three months meter rental – this is something I call whole life value, which we look at later in this book.

Compound all of this by the many thousands of individuals that have also had a rubbish experience with British Gas and it's not hard to see how a great swell of dissatisfaction manifests itself into a humdrum undertone of negative feeling towards them.

Not so sure? As I put together the finishing touches to this publication British Gas is in the news again, this time having been fined £2.5m for poor customer service.

I have read various articles on the subject and of particular note was the comment: "After a £4m investment, we are now confident we meet all of our regulatory requirements." Notice that there isn't a mention of customers or customer service here! It's as if British Gas are concerned only with doing the bare minimum necessary, rather than building a reputation for a great customer focus. Its attitude is still wrong more than 10 years later on.

Promoters

But it's not all doom and gloom, the Customer Experience Report 2006 also identified that 78% of respondents would 'greatly or somewhat' increase their custom on the basis of consistently good service. These are the people that would normally score 9 and 10 when asked how likely they were to recommend a company to their friends or colleagues, which makes them 'Promoters' on our earlier scale of loyalty groups.

Now, promoters are your perfect customers! They love you, they think you're great! They've had a great experience with you, so much so that given the opportunity they will tell everybody about it! They're very engaged with your company and enjoy the relationship they have with you because they feel special, they feel valued. And it's because of this perceived special relationship that they have with you that they are far more likely to buy other products and services from you and are much less sensitive to price than any of the other types of customers.

Everything you do should be geared to creating promoters from your customers because it is they who give you the loyal customer base on which to build your business. They are the customers that will come back and buy from you time and time again, recommend you to family and friends and experiment with you when you want to try something different. They forgive you your minor faults and errors and look to see only the best from your business. They appreciate value for money and are your most profitable segment of customers.

OK, but how do you get your customers to be promoters?

Well first off you follow the Golden Rule of building positive relationships with your customers...

• Show them you value their business!

You have to treat them as if they're important, as if they're a really valuable commodity to you – which indeed they are!

Funnily enough this may be far more difficult than you imagine. You see customers don't want to be just another statistic on a database, part of the mill and throng, the great unwashed, the hoi polloi or whatever you want to call them.

We all know that in many instances that we are of infinitesimal value to a large organisation turning over many billions of pounds but we actually want our business to be valued no matter how small it may be. I know that when I buy a sandwich from Tesco that my contribution here to their overall profit must be too minute to calculate but that doesn't stop me from wanting a fresh, quality product. In fact even my weekly shop at Tesco must be negligible compared to the businesses overall turnover, yet they have been able to achieve something that I believe is quite impressive.

For me Tesco are a brilliant organisation but supermarkets are quite an emotive subject and everybody has their favourite – wow, there I've said it – we all have a favourite supermarket. Just think about that, I mean supermarkets are all the same aren't they? They all pretty much sell the same things in the same type of store in the same places. They all lay out their stores pretty much in the same fashion and the staff that work there all wear pretty much the same type of uniform.

So when you think about it we really shouldn't have a preference for a supermarket one way of the other, but yet we all do. So how is it that the supermarkets have not only been able to differentiate themselves from each other but have also managed to create customer loyalty ahead of their competitors?

There's no one answer to this question and the big four supermarkets have whole teams of specialist people whose job it is to build this brand loyalty – not through any one specific grand initiative but through hundreds of sometimes miniscule ideas that combine to create a great overall customer experience, almost undiscernibly. This goes back to our sausage exercise that we went through much earlier in this book.

But where the supermarkets really pull all the stops out is with their loyalty club cards and reward schemes. These are particularly important to supermarkets because when you use your club card you help the supermarket profile your shopping habits. They build a picture of your shopping traits, what you buy and how often and this helps them select the offers they send you each month with your statement.

Now for me this is really clever because they are able to achieve the sense of having a personal attention and interest in their customers by tailoring the offers they make to the customers' shopping pattern. For example, if part of your regular shopping routine is the purchase of frozen pizza then the supermarket will tailor its special offers to include at some point a frozen pizza offer. In fact all of the offers I receive from my local Tesco are for things that I generally buy on a regular basis and I'm really delighted.

Why? Well it wasn't so long ago that retailers and supermarkets would send you offers for whatever it was that they wanted to sell that particular month. Quite often these offers would be for things that I would never buy or could never use and so to me it was quite obvious that they weren't interested in me as a customer. Nowadays these supermarket businesses employ supercomputers that measure every minute detail of their business including profiling each and every one of their loyalty card members.

Now some of you will be allergic to the fact that the supermarkets are building vast databases defining your shopping habits to the point that they could probably predict your next week's shopping better than you can – but for me I think it's great! I'm impressed that they value their customers so much that they would go to the trouble of investing in a system that helps them to give their customers a better service (OK, I guess there's a big profit angle here but the spinoff is a much better approach towards the customer).

I'm chuffed that they would give me special offers on things that they know I'm already going to buy – I mean they don't have to, I'm going to buy them anyway right? So why give away money when they don't have to?

Well the answer is simple, these businesses are working for their customers. They are not content just meeting their expectations, they are constantly striving to exceed them and the results are clear to see – internet shopping, shop and drop, personalised special offers, non-food goods, 24 hour opening, cheap fuel and the list goes on. Yes these are well-honed, refined businesses and no I don't agree with the way they sometimes behave when it comes to screwing their suppliers to the floor but there are many businesses out there that could learn a thing or two from them on how to gauge what the customer wants and react to it.

It's easy to see how you can find yourself becoming engaged with organisations like these and I guess that's why we each have our own favourite supermarket. I am also sure there are many other businesses out there that are just as deserving of your custom and loyalty as your favourite supermarket and these will no doubt have worked just as hard to build your loyalty – but there are equally major brands that don't show any interest in their customers and value them only for the money they bring and not their greater worth to the business.

Passives/neutrals

Passives are customers whose experience was OK but nothing to write home about. These are the people that bought something from you and whose experience was satisfactory but could not be considered to exceed expectation.

They visited your premises or used your service – it wasn't rubbish, but it wasn't brilliant either – it was 'just ok'.

The problem with being 'just ok' is that it does nothing to engender customer loyalty. Passive customers can take you or leave you, and are just as likely to do the latter!

For me, passives are the most important section of your customer base because these are the customers you are most likely to lose to your competitors. Now you might think that strange and argue that 'detractors' – those customers who are negative about our businesses – are the ones we are most likely to lose – not so.

Once we are aware of customer dissatisfaction we can take steps to address issues raised and in doing so convert our customers to 'promoters' – there's more on this in the next chapter.

Passives on the other hand are much less likely to give us feedback, after all what is there to say? This means that it's harder to engage them in the business and harder still to find opportunities to exceed expectation once they have left. In my experience passives form the biggest part of my clients' customer base and this is something that always concerns me.

Don't be fooled into thinking that by meeting your customers' expectations or having satisfied customers you are building a loyal customer base, you are not. Meeting expectations is nothing to crow about especially if the expectations weren't particularly high in the first place. And as far as satisfaction is concerned, I never want my customers to be satisfied, I want them to be delighted!

NPS™ Score

So the chaps at Baine Institute and Fred Reichfeld looked at how a business' customer base could be broken down into these three key sectors (detractors, passives and promoters) and devised a formula from which to measure improvement.

It's a particularly simple formula that takes the percentage of customers that are detractors and deducts them from the percentage of promoters, as shown below. Passives don't get a look in here as they don't influence your reputation one way or the other.

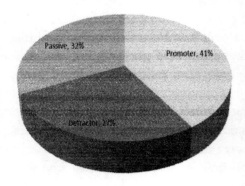

So in this illustration we can see that our customer base contains 41% promoters, 32% passives and 27% detractors – so when we calculate our NPS™ score we subtract the percentage of detractors from the percentage of promoters – so in the example above:

Promoters	41%
less	
Detractors	27%
NPS™	14

So the range for your NPS™ score can be anywhere between –100 to +100 and there are various benchmark scores available for different industry sectors.

I really like the simplicity of this metric, our American cousins call the survey the 'Ultimate Question' and I guess in some ways it is. But perhaps the most powerful compelling argument for NPS™ comes from the simplicity of just one metric score to work by. When you consider the many varying and infinite Key Performance Indicators (KPI) a business measures one can imagine the division of resource and management experience required to influence them all – yet with NPS™ there is only one metric and only one point of focus.

My own experience of this is entirely positive and so is that of my clients, all of whom are experiencing positive changes and growth in their companies. But don't necessarily take my word for it, plenty of studies have been undertaken on this particular subject and I'm going to share some of the findings of the London School of Economics (LSE) who produced a white paper entitled 'Advocacy Drives Growth' – here are some of their findings:

- For the average business they analysed they were able to show that every 1 point increase in their NPS™ score equated to nearly £9m in creased sales
- An increase of 7 points in NPS™ equated to a 1% increase in growth
- Reducing negative NPS by 1% also increased revenues by as much as £24.8m, with every 2% reduction in NPS™ showing a 1% increase in growth
- Taking everything into consideration the LSE discovered that businesses that had relatively high positive NPS™ scores combined with a low level of negative NPS™ scores grew 4 times as fast as their contemporaries.

Wow, pretty convincing stuff! Of course their study was carried out on the early adopters of NPS™, which tended to be the large UK corporations such as Lloyds TSB, Sainsbury's, FIAT and T-Mobile but nevertheless the results are striking.

In fact NPS™ is one of the very few metrics that has been proven to make a financial impact on a business' bottom line profit. We use it as the key metric in our organisation and it is the key driver for our online feedback system — Your Impressions™.

However, I urge caution here, don't forget that an NPS™ score is just a number and behind that number there is a real live customer whose individual experience counts. Whilst your NPS™ score is a great steer for you, the only real way to influence it is to create a business that focuses on delivering a consistently great customer experience. Engage each one of your customers through feedback, react and manage their concerns and show them that you value their business.

You have to have a business that's driven towards the customer experience in every way, don't just rely on the quality of your products or services and expect them to compensate for failings elsewhere because they don't. I'll try to explain what I mean by sharing with you my experiences with Mercedes Benz.

I have been a Mercedes driver for nearly 20 years and like most Mercedes drivers we adore the cars but find the business inadequate — it's our love of the cars that drives us to sometimes overlook the minor indiscretions of the dealer even when they're not so minor, but only for so long.

Let me tell you about my experiences with Mercedes Benz and their dealers over my time as a Mercedes driver. None of which has been particularly good – in fact I can honestly say that my only positive experience of Mercedes Benz has been behind the wheel.

I'm not really sure where to start. I suppose I could tell you about the time I waited three months for a special hands free kit for my Merc convertible (in the days before bluetooth), which when fitted looked like part of the original trim only for the dealer to leave it in the box and use four ruddy great bolts to attach it to the central console sticking out like a bloomin' electricity pylon.

This was particularly distressing because I distinctly remember having a quite specific discussion with my 'customer service advisor', warning him in no uncertain terms that if he drilled my car that I would come down to the workshop and drill his head (I think it is important to note that I had no intention of carrying out my threats and used the turn of phrase to emphasise the point that he should be careful when fitting the hands free kit). So you would think that with a very specific instruction and carefully constructed reminder that he would have taken extra care not to 'drill' my car – hmmm, you'd think.

Anyway, one brand new replacement central consul later and we're back on an even keel for a while. A year or two after that and a different Mercedes is in the workshop for a service – late in the day I arrive to collect my car. Now many dealers like to take you through this defined process that they have to give you back your car. This usually involves a cup of coffee, a sit down and a run through of bill. I guess the thinking is that if you're nice and comfy you're much less likely to question the bill, who knows?

Anyhow, I'm listening but not really listening to the customer service advisor as he explains to me which bits have been replaced and what work they've done and everything is as I thought it would be until I start to run through the bill myself and come across an item marked screen wash - £3.

"What's this about screen wash?" I ask.

"Oh, it's part of our service, we always put screen wash in the car," he replied.

"But it doesn't need any screen wash, I filled it the day before yesterday."

"Oh, don't worry," he said, "we only used a bit and put the rest in the boot of your car."

"But it doesn't need any screen wash," I said.

It was at this point that it went quiet, I don't suppose this sort of thing happened very often and the customer service advisor didn't really know how to handle it. I expect that most of his customers would have just accepted this unnecessary expense I mean after all it was only £3 right?

Well no, how come I end up paying £3 for a bottle of screen wash that I didn't need in the first place. And where does the dealer get off charging me £3 for a bottle of screen wash when I've just coughed up nearly £500 for a service. I have to tell you that if I gave my customer a bill for £500 I would be too embarrassed to itemise screen wash at £3 – come on, you would just give it to them right?

And this is exactly why I'm so annoyed. I'm annoyed because some half-wit bean cruncher has worked out that if they up sell a bottle of screen wash every time they service a car they'll make an extra something thousand pounds a year – how short sighted is that!

Now I've had this argument many times with many different people and yes, I recognise that the dealer has to make a profit, but the way to do this is to build customer loyalty, not by trying to sneak an extra couple of quid on each invoice. Remember customers that are engaged with your company are much less sensitive to price and will pay more to deal with you rather than your competitors, and how do you get your customers to engage with you? Well for starters, how about chucking in a free bottle of screen wash with every service!

So I hope I've made my point, charging me for a bottle of screen wash on a £500 bill when I didn't need it was a bad move. Just because I might be one of the few people that can actually be bothered to mention it doesn't mean that I'm the only one to notice. Sadly, things only got worse...

After the silence became unbearable the customer service advisor finally gathered up the wherewithal to ask me what I wanted to do about it. Naturally I told him to take it off the bill. So, somewhat sheepishly he walked into the office behind him where I could hear him discussing the problem with his colleague.

Now, it's pretty obvious that changing their bill for a £3 bottle of screen wash was probably a lot of aggro and that was the whole point in making them do it. Problem was that it was all within earshot and I could hear a somewhat miffed service manager do his best to wriggle out of it including suggesting offering me a credit note.

"Don't want a credit note,", I said clearly, so that they knew I could hear them and some minutes later the customer service advisor walked out of the office with my newly prepared bill minus a £3 bottle of screen wash. Just when I thought I was done with this shower of incompetence the customer service advisor proceeded to tell me that their jet wash machine had broken down so that they weren't able to clean my car for me (which of course translated into "we couldn't be bothered to wash your car even though you've just paid us £500").

Do you know what? I couldn't be bothered to argue the toss, I had had enough for one day and walked out to the car park to collect my car, which having been parked under a tree all day was covered in bird lime – the camel's back had broken.

It's fair to say that once I had finished tearing a strip off the customer service advisor I proceeded to dish out the same treatment to the dealer principle, who once again apologised that their jet wash had broken – I asked him if he knew what a bucket and sponge was.

By way of apology he provided me with a full valet for my car, which I have to say was very good but by then the relationship was sullied and in need of desperate attention. Sadly things only got worse, experiences too numerous to mention but ones that I can summarise quite simply.

Mercedes Benz have taken no interest in me personally, they have never showed that they have valued my business and despite the fact that I have had a major falling out with them have continued to mail or call me with special offers. All this and I got rid of my Mercedes some months ago, not that they would notice. So here I am telling you – don't buy a Mercedes, the cars are great but Mercedes Benz UK and their dealer network have no interest in their customers other than what they can get out of them. Why else would one dealer quote £295 for a service and another £900 for the very same procedure?

Thing is I'm sure my experience with Mercedes Benz isn't the only poor one, just as I am sure that there will be many people out there that have had a good if not fabulous experience with the company (although I have yet to meet one) but this is all irrelevant.

The fact is that my bad experience causes me to dissuade as many people as I can from buying a Mercedes and this is the principle of word-of-mouth buzz. It doesn't actually matter that I no longer have a Mercedes, my opinion of them hasn't changed and it's likely that I will continue to pass negative comments about them for some time to come. Of course I'm just one individual and my share of voice in the thousands of others that form the undercurrent of word-of-mouth is probably negligible. But that's the thing I'm probably not the only voice of dissent and when there's enough of us that voice becomes heard and it will have a very negative impact on the company indeed.

Building customer affinity and loyalty – The Golden Rule

What we've learnt so far is that the customer experience needs your full, absolute and undivided attention and that it's very easy to lose a grip of this with so many things to go wrong.

But what aspects of the customer experience should you focus on? Where should we look to create a great customer experience? Well this is going to differ for you all dependent on what you do and which market sector you're in.

However there is some good news and I can give you a very positive steer in the right direction with my one, simple Golden Rule: "If you want to create loyal customers you need only show them that you value their business!"

Now this can be relatively easy to achieve if you're a small business but a lot harder when you have tens if not hundreds of thousands of customers – but not impossible, think back to how the supermarkets do it.

Through simple, targeted, customer centric offers they are able to show their customers that they're interested in them (they know what each of their customers buys) and this in turn enables them to show that they value their custom (they provide relevant offers on the regular products that each of their customers buys, even when they don't have to) – so in very simplistic terms they are able to demonstrate their understanding of this Golden Rule.

I would like to explore the Golden Rule with you in a little more detail but before we do so I want to go back to the subject of customer surveys and questionnaires. The reason for this is that asking your customers for feedback is a great way to show that you're interested in them and that you value their business, providing that you do it in the right way.

- Address your customers personally using their name
- Let them decide what they want to tell you – no tick boxes here
- Make sure if the survey is connected to a recent purchase or communication and that you acknowledge this in detail
- And any issues raised, right away.

Let me cover a particular point relating to the way you show your customer you value them – this is about effort.

How many of you have had your car serviced only to receive a survey in the post and the very first thing of which they ask you is what your registration number is or what work you just had done? Errr – OK? Didn't you just service my car? Don't you know what the registration number is? Don't you know what work you just did? And there are plenty of other examples such as the holiday firm whose first question was which resort did you visit? Come on, you arranged the trip didn't you? Don't you remember?

Of course they do, but they haven't changed their internal processes to allow them to capture all the relevant data to send out their survey properly – probably because they couldn't be bothered. After all isn't it easier just to let the customer fill in all that detail?

Well it might be for them, but as a customer it sucks. It sucks because they couldn't be bothered to do it right in the first place and it sucks because it shows that I'm not that important enough to them to do it right. Still I've seen worse, especially those surveys that are addressed to Mr Dolcezza, which later ask what sex I am?!!

But assuming you do it right, using an open survey is a great way of showing your customer that you're interested enough in them to value their opinion. In fact for me it's the starting point in any relationship you have with your customer – after all how can you tailor your offering to them if you don't know what appeals? How can you make things better if you don't know what's wrong? Engaging the customer in feedback is a vital part of showing you're interested in them and it's a fabulous way to establish how interested they are in you!

What we're trying to achieve here is engagement, a building of relationships through interaction – but engagement is not always positive. Customers are normally engaged with your business because they have either had a great experience or a bad experience but either way it's all good.

OK, you're asking how come a customer who has had a bad experience is a good thing? The answer is because if you know about a problem you have the opportunity to do something about it and this means that you have the opportunity to turn a negative customer (a detractor as mentioned earlier) into a positive promoter. When we do this we create what I have termed as a positive loop of affirmation, which looks a little like this:

When a customer makes the decision to buy a product or service from you they do so based on their good judgement. In effect they have weighed up the pros and cons of buying from you such as price and service, factored in what they know of you and what they've heard, and made a pro-active decision to select you as their supplier. Now this happens for every purchase to some degree or another, and most of the time without the conscious thought of the purchaser, however without some form of positive advocacy it's very unlikely they will buy.

When things go wrong following a purchase decision the customer's judgement in choosing you as a supplier is brought into question. This has a very negative effect on a subconscious level, because it means that the decision to buy was flawed and being flawed is something we would all rather avoid. So when things go wrong we draw to attention the flawed decision and that creates negative advocacy – a detractor!

For me the true worth of a company isn't gauged when everything is perfect, it's gauged when things go wrong. Only when things do not go as expected do we get a real sense of how good a company is. It's here where we get to see just how important we are as customers.

Remember, customers don't expect things to be perfect but they do expect you to put things right when they go wrong and it's how you do this that has the effect of changing a customer from a negative detractor to a positive promoter. Acting quickly is essential and as important as being effective, make a positive decision to put things right quickly and you will have reminded the customer that choosing you in the first place was the right decision – but you need to go further.

Remember that our objective here is to show the customer that we value them and their business. Putting things right is the very least our customer will expect of us and if that's all we do we will have only met their expectation. To truly show that we value their business we need go even further.

I would like to recount to you a story of a client of mine working in the hospitality industry who happened to collar me one day as I was passing through his office. He wanted to ask me my opinion on a difficult problem he had with a corporate customer. It turns out that he and his team had dropped the ball and the poor old client got much less than he deserved or bargained for.

Now my client was by no means a dummy and had already offered a 70% refund to his customer but it would seem that this wasn't enough.

"So whose fault was it that things went wrong?" I asked.

"Ah – well I have to admit that we were in the wrong".

"So why haven't you refunded all of your customer's money?" I asked him.

"Well," came the reply, "if I retain this 30% then I won't be out of pocket."

"No, but you will be one customer less," I tried to persuade him.

"So what do you think I should do?"

"I think you should give your customer a full refund, apologise profusely and give him a 10% discount on his next booking – and I think you should do it right now!"

"Ok," he said not at all convinced, "I won't hold it against you if it doesn't pan out."

Now some months later I received a telephone call from my client to tell me that his customer had just booked conference and catering facilities to the tune of £15,000 –he was a little sheepish, perhaps expecting me to say: "I told you so!"

In this instance giving back part or even all of the customer's booking fee wasn't enough, he needed to show the customer that he was sorry and that he valued their business and to do that he needed to go so that extra step and give the additional discount. Only then did he show the customer that they were truly important to him.

What's important is that you have vindicated the customer's decision to buy from you in the first place. It's this which creates a greater affinity between your customer and your business. You see a customer that has firsthand experience of how well you handle problems when they arise is more secure in their relationship with you. This is because the fear of the unknown in terms of what they can expect from your customer service has dissipated. The customer is able to draw on their previous experiences with you to predict how well they will be looked after going forward.

In fact a number of studies, including the one carried out by the LSE, have identified that these customers, the ones that have endured a negative experience then put right, have a far greater affinity with the company than those that have just had a good experience. Quite often cementing a relationship with such a degree of loyalty and affinity that they quite literally become a customer for life.

Nowadays my client has a great perspective on customers that give negative feedback or make complaints – he loves them. For the most part this is because he has learnt and developed the skills to deal with these people, grievances don't scare him, in fact he positively thrives on them. He sees them as a personal challenge, an opportunity to reverse a disappointed and sometimes angry customer into a loyal and engaged one. This isn't magic, sure he uses skills that help him deal with an irate customer, but his success is due to the fact that he is genuinely interested in the customer and makes a determined effort to resolve the customer's issues.

Remember, customers aren't stupid – they will see and recognise that he is genuinely interested in their predicament and is taking personal responsibility for getting matters resolved. He doesn't abdicate responsibility by passing the buck to some poor sap in the customer service department like many other weak and ineffective managers, he takes it on the chin and deals with it.

Of course none of this could happen if the customer wasn't invited to give feedback in the first place and many disgruntled customers never get the opportunity to express their feelings and ultimately vote with their feet.

So engaging your customers through feedback is a good way to show that you're interested in them, but in my experience the feedback you get will in the main be from those customers that have had either a very good experience or a very bad one. Customers that had a mediocre or average experience don't normally bother to provide feedback – in essence they have nothing to say, it wasn't a bad experience but neither was it particularly good.

And that's the problem. It's almost impossible to get feedback from customers who have simply had their expectation met, although not surprising. Let me explain what I mean with this example. I happened to visit B&Q, the national hardware store chain. I was looking for a de-humidifier as we have a particularly old house that is prone to the odd spot of damp. The store was nice, I remember it being an especially spacious store, but then again it was only recently built. As we walked in we were able to walk straight up the first aisle and easily catch the attention of one of the two staff engaged in chat.

I asked where we could find the item I wanted and he gave me clear directions – he didn't walk me directly to the shelf as they tend to do at the supermarket, but I wasn't disappointed by this as his directions were easy to follow and took me straight to where I wanted to go. I picked up my de-humidifier from the shelf and carried it to the check out. I noticed for the first time that they had installed the self service tills that had become so popular with the national supermarket chains. As I made my way to the manned checkout I could clearly hear an automated message coming from the self service till encouraging all customers to leave their feedback "details on the reverse of your receipt" I heard it say.

Supporting this audible message there were countless pieces of point of sale merchandise designed to achieve the same thing. Finally, once I had paid for my goods and was leaving through the exit doors I saw the most prominent message of all 'win £1,000' and then on reading further I could see that this was a key incentive, a last gasp chance to get the customer to think about leaving some feedback and a web address where they could do this.

Now here am I, a feedback survey freak that looks at any and every survey that any company is doing not at least to see what businesses are up to – but this time I just couldn't be bothered.

But then why would I?

I went to the B&Q store, I knew what I wanted and I found it easy enough – I paid for it and I left. So there it is, nothing special, it wasn't rubbish but it wasn't anything to write home about either and that's just the point. There was nothing going on that made my experience particularly special. There was nothing that the store or the staff did to make me feel that they were interested in me or really valued my business. Don't get me wrong, I've had way worse purchasing experiences than this one and really have no complaints here but in the loyalty stakes I have no more loyalty to B&Q now than I did when I bought my dehumidifier.

And that's just not good for business.

Businesses need customer loyalty to grow. They need the continued custom from their existing customers while they look to win new customers to their brand. Failure to do this means missing out on growth, worse still if businesses lose existing customers faster than they are winning new customers their company is in danger of decline.

Many of you will recognise this more simply as a matter of market share but I think its much more than that. Market share just isn't a strong enough term to explain what's actually going on. It gives the impression of a clinical un-emotive statistic that represents a business' standing in its chosen market – and so it does. But more to the point it's a reflection of the customer loyalty trend. Losing market share means that your customers are switching their loyalties to your competitors and that's not at all clinical or un-emotive, it's very personal indeed!

It's personal because we know that customers switch loyalty when they feel that their supplier isn't interested in them or they don't feel that their custom is valued, in effect the business has failed to engage with their customers. Believe me, this happens all the time and it's happened to me quite recently.

Up until a short while ago I was a Tesco man through and through. I wouldn't shop anywhere else and never had any need to – that was until, like any business,

Tesco started tweaking with its product range. Now I don't know whether I was unlucky or whether all their customers were having the same experience but it seemed to me that more and more of the products I used to buy regularly were being dropped from the range or being replaced by other lesser quality brands. In some instances the most heinous of all supermarket follies would occur where Tesco replaced a product that I had happily being buying for many years with their own inferior brand that neither looked nor tasted the same.

Thing is with loyalty that you overlook one or two of these misdemeanours and stick with your favourite supplier. After all you've been through it together – for better or for worse you have looked after each other and so the odd change here and there gets put to one side, but never forgotten.

I say never forgotten because every time I visit my local Tesco I'm reminded when I look at the shelf that they no longer stock the item or brand that I used to buy. But this isn't really good for Tesco because eventually my visit was more memorable for the things that I used to be able to buy but can't get anymore – at least not from Tesco.

So I find myself visiting Sainsbury's more often as they still stock several items that I like that I just can't get from Tesco. Until eventually the position shifts to the point where it is easier for me to go to Sainsbury's for my regular shop than it is to Tesco and so before you know it, almost by stealth, my loyalty has switched.

And this is an example of market share changing but this change isn't built on special offers, price or even on the product range, it's built on shifting loyalties. Tesco have failed with me because they forgot the Golden Rule – if they had valued my business they could have done more to manage my expectations. Their Clubcard systems would have showed them the products I bought regularly and so they would have known that a change in product range would have affected my purchasing experience. Yet they did nothing to lessen the impact or even apologise for it.

Now don't get me wrong, I am just one customer. And I recognise that Tesco is a business. As such they need to behave in a manner that generates profits and that from time to time this may mean a change in the product range. As a loyal customer I would accept that. At least I would if they treated me as a loyal customer and with a little more consideration, especially as I know that they can. So some of you will be saying that I'm being daft and that I shouldn't possibly expect a company the size of Tesco to be so fastidious about caring for my own particular desires and needs. Well I say phooey to you!

Whether or not we care to admit it or whether we are even aware of it, all customers build their supplier loyalties on the back of the Golden Rule. This means that whether it's one customer or one million customers the approach must be the same – after all what is a million customers other than a million people just like me. A million individuals with their own desires and needs and a million customers that can switch their loyalties just as I have done. Don't mistake the importance of the individual, that's what being customer centric is all about.

What this tells us is that it's not hard keeping a loyal customer. Loyal customers will forgive you minor indiscretions. They'll turn a blind eye to the occasional bad service or faulty product and they'll stick with you for as long as you can show them that you're interested in them and that you value their custom. And you really do have to go a long way to get to the point of losing a loyal customer and when you do, you need to recognise it for what it is – a monumental failure.

But let's just assume that you get the gist of this and you're going to work really hard at looking after your loyal customers. The next thing you're going to want to do is to build your business off the back of this loyalty by winning new customers to your company and in turn making these new customers as equally loyal to your business, but how?

Well for me it's relatively straight forward and merely meeting customer expectations just doesn't cut it. I expect every business I buy from to meet my expectations, that's why I chose them in the first place. I mean if my expectation was to receive a rubbish product or poor service I simply wouldn't go there would I? If I thought for one moment that the service I was going to get in B&Q was going to be anything less than acceptable, I would have chosen to buy my goods from elsewhere as I have done with hundreds of companies on hundreds of occasions.

And so when I walked into that store I had a clear picture in my head of how the experience would go and unless that experience in reality was markedly different to how I imagined, it would be entirely unnoticeable – and so it was. In fact if I had chosen to write this section a year or two from now, I may well have forgotten about my experience and used some other example to illustrate my point.

So, in order to get my attention my experience has to be markedly different to the one I had imagined it would be. Now generally this only happens when the experience goes horribly wrong and I have given you plenty of examples of this. But only rarely does it exceed my expectations. The companies that do, tend to be extremely successful and it's not hard to see why.

Let me tell you about my experience with Dyson, the well-known vacuum cleaner manufacturer. Buying my Dyson wasn't anything special, in fact I can't even remember which retailer I bought it from. It's post purchase where I really got the benefit of the fabulous Dyson service.

We had owned the vacuum for quite a while, I'm not sure how long, but it would have been more than a year when we had a recurring problem that would see the unit cut out after only a few minutes use. Not great and almost impossible to get the vacuuming done. So I went on to the internet and looked on the Dyson website and found a contact number of the Dyson service centre.

Now I can't be sure whether Dyson run their own service centre or whether they outsource it to a third party provider, but I would have to say based on their 'ownership' of my experience that I am almost certain that they operate their own internal facility. The call operator was very helpful and even though I had failed to send in my warranty registration (as I never do, wouldn't it be nice if the retailer did this for you!) she was able to identify from the serial number which retailer took stock of my Dyson and when. From that she could verify that my unit was still under warranty and dispatched a service engineer to call within a couple of days.

She was extremely helpful and went out of her way to help me as much as possible and I really did get the sense that nothing was too much trouble. I felt valued as a Dyson customer. This set the scene nicely, for when the service engineer arrived he couldn't have been more helpful either. Not only did he replace the defective part but he also gave our vacuum a complete 'once over' replacing other parts without request and without charge! He carried out a thorough service overhaul and left me with a vacuum that felt to me as if it were brand new. And to top it all, two days later a free replacement hose arrived in the post for us to replace the one we had that was showing signs of wear, hardly surprising as we had been using it daily since we bought it more than a year earlier.

Now that's impressive – I have no doubt that the service call cost far more than it could have. The service engineer need only to have replaced the defective part, instead he carried out a complete overhaul and changed parts that were showing signs of wear or looking that they might fail at some point in the future. I was so impressed by the level of service offered by Dyson that I will never buy another brand of vacuum again, they have my undivided loyalty. But there's far more to this Dyson customer service strategy than first meets the eye. Consider the benefits of their approach:

- Future business secured – (a totally loyal customer)
- Positive word-of-mouth advocacy – (I'm telling everyone how fabulous Dyson is, think of how many of you are reading this!)
- Preventative service carried out – (it's like fixing a chip in your wind screen before it turns into a crack that means replacing the whole thing).

I'm really impressed that some bright spark at Dyson has weighed up the benefits of a really good customer service policy on bottom line profit. And that's the whole thing about really good customer service, it comes straight back at you as increased business and great profits.

This is something I call investing in advocacy, where a business invests in the positive experience of its customers, when it need not to, for the positive advocacy that it generates – there's more on this later.

Dyson was able to see beyond the pathetic penny pinching of my local Mercedes dealer and it's £3 for a bottle of screen wash. They recognised that there is a direct link between reputation and profitability, and it is sensible enough to know that it's worth investing in a great customer experience not just for the credibility it brings. In the long run its more cost effective.

Now, let me tell you about the ridiculous, miserly experience I had with the Halifax. Now I know that the outrageous actions of our banks during the recession years have made them global pariahs, but this particular experience happened quite a while before the world turned upside down.

Yep, in the days of easy credit, the banks were literally throwing money at us! And so when the Halifax invited me to have £8k of their money for free, zip, nada for six months in exchange for me taking out one of their credit cards I thought "Yeah OK, I'll have your money, why not?" It was easy enough to apply and I transferred balances off other credit cards to my new Halifax card, rather than paying them off and got myself an extra £8k to play around with.

Now, I had every intention of paying the card off in good time so to avoid the interest charges that they would undoubtedly be applying once the card flipped over from the six month interest free period into interest bearing. However, I have to tell you that I am not the most organised individual in my personal life. The consequence of which is that I totally forgot until the day that my Halifax credit card statement arrived to tell me that I had just incurred £121 interest to my balance.

"OK, fair do's, you got me," I explained to the lady from the Halifax on the telephone.

"I totally intended to pay this balance off before the interest became due but completely forgot." I quipped like a naughty school boy. "Could I please have a settlement figure as I want to pay off this card completely – there's no chance I'm going to get caught out again on this one next month."

Now I vaguely remember the lady on the telephone muttering something about interest being calculated daily, but in all honesty I wasn't paying much attention. I just wanted to clear the balance on this card in order to avoid the costly interest charges – and as far as I was concerned that's exactly what I did, or so I thought.

Low and behold, the following month I received a credit card statement from the Halifax and imagine my surprise to see that I had an outstanding balance of 53p! I have to say that I was probably more annoyed than surprised and so I got on the telephone straight away to have it out with them.

The chap I got to speak to was less than helpful and I don't suppose it helped that I was a bit miffed at their ineptitude but he wasn't very forthcoming either. I explained to him the situation and that I had asked the previous operator that I wished to settle the outstanding balance on my account and here I was with a 53p bill in effect.

At this point he tried to explain to me that the previous operator was unable to give me an accurate settlement figure as interest is charged to my account daily and her systems didn't permit her an up-to-date daily figure.

Of course I explained to him that I had no interest whatsoever in the shortcomings of the Halifax computer systems and that as far as I was concerned I had settled the outstanding balance and that was an end of it.

Sadly it wasn't.

My call operator told me that despite settling over £8,000 the previous month the settlement figure I was given was only an estimate and that the 53p remaining is correct and due.

It was at this point that I suggested that it would be in the best interest of us both and a great customer relations exercise if he was to write off the 53p and leave me with a zero balance. He declined.

And so, as seems to happen often at this point, I got a little narked, in fact I got really cheesed off. I told my call operator that while I still had breath I was never, ever going to pay the Halifax this 53p and that if he wanted it so badly he would have to take me to court!

As calmly as he could muster he replied: "Well that's up to you sir."

"Yes it is," I said and hung up.

Now at this point I was fairly confident that someone at Halifax would see sense and just write it off. Certainly I could not envisage a court summons for such a paltry amount so I just parked the whole experience and forgot about it – until my next monthly statement arrived.

More intrigued than annoyed, I opened my statement to reveal an outstanding balance of 53p plus 1p interest added – my new balance was 54p! I mean it was just too ludicrous to be true. It didn't take a genius to work out that in postage and printing alone the expense of sending me this statement was many times more than the 1p interest added.

And so I did nothing.

And every month for a good while after Halifax would send me a statement adding 1p interest to my outstanding balance until I had amassed a huge £1.19 debt. It was only now that someone in Halifax had cottoned on to the cost of sending out statements with such small balances on them and a change of policy meant a change to the way interest was applied to an account with a minimum charge of 50p added each month.

For many months now I had my monthly dose of enjoyment when receiving my Halifax statement but this change in policy was a sign that perhaps after many, many months that the time for such mirth had passed. So with a heavy heart I contacted the Halifax in order to attempt to resolve the matter again.

This time and by complete contrast my operator couldn't have been more helpful. He was polite and charming and very obliging. I explained the whole story from way back when and how unhelpful the last chap had been and how the lack of sensibility on the part of the Halifax had probably cost them over £20 in unnecessary mailings.

I think he saw the funny side, but apologised kindly anyway and set about immediately cancelling the card and wiping off the outstanding balance – so in the matter of no more than two minutes the matter was resolved and everything was back to normal, leaving me with the question why wasn't it that easy the first time around? Well by now I hope that you have a pretty good idea of why – Halifax had put business process ahead of customer satisfaction.

Now, if you're Mr Halifax Bank you're more than likely moaning about my criticism of your business. You probably want to make it known that you have changed your business process to be much more customer-focused and that the business is far better all around. Well Mr Halifax Bank it may well be, but it took you way too long to do it! And in all that time, I shared my rubbish experience with your bank with anyone who would care to listen.

I think it goes without saying that I wouldn't ever put the Halifax on my list of potential banks next time I go looking for one and even though my last experience with them was better, things went beyond the point of no return.

And I guess that's a point of significance we ought to bear in mind. When you cock up and I mean you really cock up, it's unlikely that you will be able to retrieve the situation. Just take heart from the fact that you truly do have to go a long way to really cock up. Generally it's got to be a catalogue of monumental disasters to push a customer beyond the point of no return. If you want to avoid this always make sure you give your customers the easiest possible opportunity to tell you when things are going wrong before they get out of hand. Make it easy for them to tell you, listen to what they are saying and react.

I'll give you more on handling disgruntled customers a little later but for now I want to get back to the point we started with, which was how to build loyalty in customers where none exists. How does B&Q get me from being a casual customer using them when it suits to be a loyal customer choosing them as a preference?

Well the golden rule is essential for this and it's not just about generating loyalty once you have a customer that's engaged with you. To get them there in the first place you need to exceed their expectations. You need to get outside of that mind map the customer has of how they expect the purchase to go and deliver them something beyond that. OK, how you ask?

That's going to depend on what your business is and what your customers expect, but whatever you do doesn't necessarily need to be costly. It could be something as simple as a smile or personally guiding a customer to a product, or it could be free canapés while your customer waits for their table. Whatever it is it needs to be something that your customer didn't expect – something that makes you stand out from the crowd and gives your customers something to talk about. It's about going the extra mile to give great service and make your customers remember you – more on this in the exceeding expectations chapter later in this book.

B&Q really are doing as much as they can to get their customers to give them feedback but it's not going to happen in any meaningful way as their customers are just not engaged with the company. Let me put it this way, if B&Q can't get me to leave them feedback (given the feedback junky that I am) what hope have they of getting feedback from the average customer?

So the first step to customer loyalty is getting the customer engaged with your company. Once you've achieved this (and don't forget customers can be engaged with you as a result of a bad experience) you can start the process of generating feedback.

Where possible, invite all of your customers to provide you with feedback. If your business captures customers' contact details then you should invite each customer personally to give you feedback. If you're a retailer it's often not possible to achieve this but good point of sale materials strategically placed will ensure that your customers are aware of how easy it is and where to provide feedback. Nowadays a big proportion of the population carry about with them all the technology you need to capture live meaningful feedback in the guise of a smart telephone. We do something really clever with this including GPS and QR codes (two dimensional bar codes) to capture feedback, live, real time, with these devises.

Be customer centric about this process as far as you can and remember customer feedback should be about what the customer wants to tell you, not what you want to know about your business. Look back at the section on customer feedback if you want a refresher.

Once we've done this we can see how much feedback we get and in doing so get a feel for how engaged our customers are with our business. For example, a small percentage of customers giving you feedback is an indication of how well or not you're doing with engaging your customers to your company. If we get a 5% response rate to our feedback invitation then 95% of our customers haven't been engaged enough with our company to be bothered to give feedback. But low response levels are in themselves good news. Firstly because they tell us that we're not particularly good at engaging customers and, secondly, they give us a bench point through which to measure our strategies for improvement going forward.

What we do with the feedback is as equally important as engaging with the customer in the first place. In fact, I would go so far as to say you're better off not asking for feedback rather than asking for feedback and not doing anything with it, particularly when the customer has a complaint.

Equally if someone takes the time to feedback compliments, you should take the time to thank them. This shows that you're interested in them and value their business and this will strengthen your relationship further and build loyalty. You should also use the feedback to learn about and build on your successes.

Remember the positive loop of affirmation means that when you put something right for your customer in a quick and efficient way you re-affirm their decision to buy from you in the first place – you endorse that decision and support it with clear actions to prove it. That's why customers that do experience problems are stronger advocates for your company than those that have just had a good experience – providing of course that you have put things right.

Now get this and remember it – negative feedback, no matter how damming, is good for your business. It's good because it highlights areas of your business where your process lets you down. It's good because once you are able to see where you are failing you are able to make positive changes to the way in which you operate. Better than all of this is the fact that your customer is giving you the opportunity to address the issues they have raised – giving you the chance not only to keep them as a customer but also to make them a positive advocate for your company.

It's also essential that you give your customers the avenue they need to sound off, to air their grievances and to make themselves heard. Otherwise you risk them finding other ways like forums, among other things to achieve this.

So we started this chapter talking about adopting the golden rule for building customer loyalty – showing your customers that you value them. To do this we've discovered that we need to understand about our customers' experiences and the best way to do this is to ask them. We recognised that we need to do this in the right way and that we need to respond to any specific issues the customer identifies.

You can value your customers by showing an interest. Taking the time to acknowledge their wants and needs – remembering who they are, what their relationship is to your business, being aware of their history with you, what they buy and what this shows us about them. Big businesses do this by profiling their customers and keeping detailed information about their purchases, and linking these to customer demographic models.

Smart smaller businesses are well-managed by super businessmen and women who work hard to remember their customers and make a concerted effort to treat them as individuals. Ultimately this is a great way of showing you're interested in your customers.

Showing your customer that you value their business is more about elevating them from being a customer to being a cherished asset. It's not about taking every opportunity to steal a margin from them, but it recognises that happy, delighted customers are usually your most profitable.

You can show that you value your customers' business in a number of ways and quite often it's the little things that count, throwaways that cost nothing but have a value in intent. A free coffee or an extra set of batteries or just asking them their opinion before you change your stock lines. It's not difficult to achieve this given a little thought – what can you do to show your customers that their business is important to you?

I can however give you a steer on things that don't work for your customers (being a customer myself). There is one particular thing that makes me cringe every time I see it and I can't for the life of me understand how major companies think of it as an acceptable marketing practice. It's the infamous 'new customers only' offers.

It beggars belief that businesses can't see that making such a statement only serves to alienate their existing customers. This is how I see it:

So, Mr Supplier, you're happy for me to continue paying what is obviously over the odds, while you offer new customers the same product/service for less money??? How can that possibly show me, as one of your existing customers, that you value my business?

This is a real dumb approach in my opinion and worse still it's normally practiced by businesses that have locked in the existing customers into some form or supply contract (e.g. a mobile phone tariff). Anybody who hears about this new, cheaper offer but is contracted to pay the old, more expensive rate is going to feel like they've been stitched up. Worse still they're going to be made to feel inadequate as shoppers, incapable of sourcing out the best deals, made to feel like a poor sap, a sucker for a glitzy offer. This is very dangerous.

This leads us back to the positive loop of affirmation we talked about earlier in this book. Remember that when a customer makes a purchase they are making a judgement call based on their experience of the product or service, the company and advice from their social networks. It's a judgement call and this means that when things go wrong your customer's judgement is being brought into question and this is distinctly personal.

Customers will often rationalise their decisions, rather than face the possibility that their judgment was flawed. For example, I can avoid feeling foolish about having paid more for my iPhone buying it from Apple than I could have paid buying it from say Comet. I do this by convincing myself that Apple are the manufacturer not just the supplier. They will be better geared to resolving any issues I raise and have more experience with the product. I rationalise these arguments as it is easier to say I paid more because I wanted to – than it is to say I paid more because I wasn't very good at shopping for this product.

But it's hard to make this rationalisation when it's the very same company that sold me my product or service as the one now selling it at a knock down rate for anybody off the street but not me! How am I expected to feel? Well, cheesed off is the answer. As an existing customer I am being told that a new customer is more important that I am – does this make me feel like my custom is valued? Of course not.

What's daft about all of this is that these companies have got this completely the wrong way around, think how different things would be if the message was:

"Only available to existing customers!"

Straight off this says we value and cherish our existing customers, so much so that we look for opportunities to show our appreciation of their loyalty.

Wow! This is a really positive statement and if I wasn't a customer of yours I would really want to be. I would really like to feel that you valued my business as much as you did your other customers. And of course anybody can take advantage of this offer just by becoming a customer. All you need to do to become a customer is to buy the product/service being offered.

I understand that businesses are always looking out for new customers, after all new customers are essential to grow your business. But it's a mistake to compromise the loyalty of your existing customer base so that you can chase new conquests. It's been known in business for as long as I can remember that it's more cost effective to keep an existing customer than it is to win a new one. If you're haemorrhaging existing customers faster than you can add new ones your business is going backwards.

Sure, put together fabulous offers to attract new customers but don't do this at the expense of your existing customers or better still make it available to them as well (without having to ask). Yep it's going to cost you money but in the long run you'll build a loyal customer base, increase your customer retention and establish yourself as a credible supplier that everyone wants to buy from (and will pay more money to do so).

But let's look at this in broader terms. What exactly does showing your customers that you value their business entail? Well to start with we need to show that we're interested in them, know them and make an effort for them. This is all the stuff we've just covered off. But we can go further to really cement our position as a preferred supplier by giving back some of the profit we earn from them. This doesn't mean that we should write them a cheque every now and then. That doesn't show that we've made any effort at all and instead we should take the time to consider how we show our appreciation for their business. Think about what products or services our customers buy from us and offer them something of value that reflects this.

One of my very first and most important clients is a fabulous businessman and great friend called Keith Brock. Keith is the Managing Director of a well respected Bristol-based car dealership group and a very insightful chap.

Keith worked out well ahead of the game that to deliver really strong dependable growth he needed to deliver fabulous customer service. He set about creating a cultural revolution within his business, moving it away from a traditional motor dealers to become a customer service business. He recognised that his team, many of whom had been with him for many years, had become fixated on business process at the expense of customer care and he became determined to change things. Among the many positive changes Keith made to his business included a number of initiatives designed to show his customers that he valued their business. One such idea was to offer all of his customers that bought a car from him a free car wash – for life! Sure enough every Saturday morning his forecourt was awash (excuse the pun) with customers queuing to get their cars cleaned. Keith knew that sooner or later they would all need to get their cars cleaned and so by offering them a free car wash he was offering them something of intrinsic value.

This idea came with masses of spin off benefits.

Firstly, Keith was able to get his customers back into his business at much more frequent intervals. This gave him the opportunity to really establish his relationship with them, building good positive advocacy that would lead to higher numbers of customers using his business not just for buying their cars but for servicing them too!

Secondly, every time they visited his business he had them as a captive audience, one that was already very amenable to him (after all they were having their car cleaned for free) and so he was able to cross sell other products and services, or just try out new ideas with these very engaged customers.

And then perhaps the most subtle benefit of all, the one that was least measureable but most important was the advocacy he was building in his community. Not only was he creating a 'buzz' in his dealership on car wash day that would have undoubtedly washed off (another pun) on new prospective car purchasers, but also in the wider populous itself.

And this is the spin off from creating great customer service, an increase in loyalty that manifests itself in your brand reputation. But just remember that wonderful famous saying: "It takes a life time to build a reputation and moments to ruin it." What this saying means is that this ethos of delivering a great customer experience is relentless, it can never stop. You can never let your guard down and you will never finish, it's the most important part of your business bar none! Let's face it, without customers you don't have a business.

Managing and exceeding customer expectations

OK, so by now we should have worked out that what we're trying to do is build a loyal customer base. We know that to achieve this we need to show the customer that we value their business.

We know that to build positive advocacy and get people talking about our company that we need to exceed expectations, create that 'wow' moment. In this chapter I'm going to talk to you about managing customer expectations and find a cost effective way to excel.

To start I want to explore with you a flawed approach that many business have towards differing levels of customer service. I touched on this earlier on when I described a motor manufacturer that wanted to reserve their very best service for buyers of the top of the range vehicles, where everybody else just got the mediocre service.

Now, not everybody agrees with me on this.

Many of you may know or be familiar with Chris Cardell, who is unquestionably one of the greatest marketing minds of our time. He is renowned for his innovative, cutting edge thinking and has helped countless businesses achieve magnificent growth through his practical advice and workshops. If you haven't seen anything from Chris then I urge you to take a look, it's pretty incredible.

In fact I have to say that Chris's advice and content have been instrumental in our own business growth and development and I pay a huge amount of credence to what he has to offer. In fact, Chris's ideas were one of the things that inspired me to write this book. I have subscribed to Chris' email, which I read regularly, and just the other day Chris broadcast an email message, which in essence was about the importance of customers to every business – can't argue with that.

However, Chris did make the following comment, which I am going to have to take issue with:

"Segment your customer list and treat the top 20% differently to the rest. For most businesses, 80% of profits come from around 20% of the customers.

Whoever wrote the book about treating all customers equally was a twit. It's nonsense. If you fly economy on Virgin, you'll be treated very well. If you fly upper class, you'll discover that Richard Branson is well aware that you don't treat all customers equally. This top 20% are your greatest protection in a turbulent economy. Treasure them."

Chris is wrong.

I bet Richard Branson would have a cow if he lost all of his economy customers to a competitor because of poor customer service. Come to think of it I don't know many businesses that wouldn't be concerned to lose 20% of their profits just because they weren't their best customers.

Sure, your most lucrative customers are probably the ones with whom you have the best relationship but it's not so hard to understand why. The volume of the work that you do with them probably demands far more of your time than customers with smaller portfolios but does this mean that you should treat them any differently?

Are you content with the number of big spending customers you have? Where do you think the next lucrative customer is going to come from if not from those smaller customers? The smaller customers that are maybe just trying you out to see how good you are before giving you that really big contract. I hear all the time from my clients who grow their business from customers who started with them really small scale.

I'm not sure that Chris is suggesting that we should give our 'lesser' customers a poor level of customer service but then what alternative is there? For me there aren't varying degrees of customer service. It's either good or bad and this is determined wholly by customer expectation.

When I buy economy flights I know I'm not going to get a three course gourmet meal. I know that my flight attendant has twice as many people to look after than those in first class and I know that this means that they're probably not going to be as attentive but all of this is OK because I wanted a cheap flight. I traded certain comforts for a cheaper ticket.

The fact is that economy and first class are two different products and therefore attract differing levels of expectation. But this doesn't mean that either warrants any less attention to customer service than the other. In fact I would argue that it will be far easier to deliver a really great customer service experience with an economy class passenger than one in first class.

Furthermore, with four times as many passengers than first class, economy are influential indeed and can easily impact on a company's brand or reputation.

I have far too much respect for Chris to call him a 'twit' but I think he's confusing customer service with sensible business priorities. The basis of his email is to give his clients advice on how to best prioritise themselves in turbulent times and I guess if you have limited resource and you're expecting to lose customers then you want to make sure that it's not the lucrative ones.

The fact of the matter is that you absolutely, positively, definitely have to treat all your customers with the same customer service ethos and that means you should always look to surpass their expectations regardless of what they spend.

Chris is great at marketing and media but he can't touch me on this, don't be persuaded otherwise by anyone.

I hope that you remember how flawed this process is and its potential impact on the businesses' reputation. It's also going to help me give you a clearer understanding of how you can exceed customer expectations and it's all down to where their relationship sits with your business.

I have quite a few legal practices as clients and I could probably describe most of them as fitting the traditional 80/20 rule – that is to say that 80% of their profit comes from 20% of their clients. Now I think it's a pretty safe bet that these 20% of clients get a spectacular level of service and would therefore be highly likely to be positive advocates, actively recommending the company to their contacts. But what about the other 80% of customers?

Well these guys are probably at the smaller end of the project scale, perhaps something simple like a will or some minor conveyancing work. Whatever the case they're unlikely to be big spenders and the nature of the work unlikely to be challenging. Quite often then, a legal firm will have lots of very efficient processes for managing these customers in the quickest and most cost-effective way. The key here is to process as efficiently as possible to maximise already meagre profits – it's the proverbial sausage machine, meat in one end and churning out finished product at the other. All very effective but not very engaging and that's a problem.

You see there are FOUR times as many of these customers getting a rather sterile relationship than there are of our very best clients. This means that there are FOUR times as many people, businesses and individuals with a rather non-plus experience of these legal practices as there are delighted customers. This is 'share of voice' and is absolutely critical to you when establishing your business reputation.

Let's also not forget that these poor clients getting only a sausage machine service could also potentially one day be one of the 20% of very best clients – well maybe they won't, I mean the service was pretty mediocre and nothing to write home about.

So this is a timely reminder about ensuring that you give every customer a great experience but what constitutes a great experience? Aha! Well that all depends on the customers' expectations. Earlier in this book I hope I was able to persuade you that all customers fundamentally have the same desires and that the only difference of consideration is the level of expectation. It's this level of expectation which offers us the best opportunity to excel. At legal practices 80% of customers that get little more than a sausage machine service probably don't expect much more than that anyway – and this is great news because it means that we don't have to break the bank (or our necks) to exceed the expectations.

Remember earlier in this book I talked about my experience at Cadbury House, a super hotel complex not far from where I live that do these absolutely fabulous chips!? Remember also that I was bowled over by these chips because I had been expecting the normal rubbish oven chips that you seem to get everywhere else. So the point is that I had my expectations exceeded by something as trivial as chips. Something as trivial as chips was able to make such an impact.

I hope that you can see that it's not necessary for you to set aside a monstrous budget to exceed customers' expectations (what was the cost of fabulous chips?). What you need to look for is the point of least expectation.

Now I'm pretty sure I said that chips alone aren't enough to make a positive advocate of me. So when you're undergoing this exercise don't restrict yourself to one or two things. Look for as many points as you can where the expectation is minimal and work with them all.

Let's translate this into positive action for our legal firm who wants to really exceed – the expectations of their 80% sausage machine customers, what should they do? Well, first they should get some understanding of what their customers' expectations are and so for this example let's assume that they have done the whole customer feedback thing and have identified what their customers expect and don't expect.

So, from my experience, I guess that the length of time it takes my legal firm to complete the transaction is going to be a problem, it always takes longer than expected. I expect that I will have to chase the solicitor as to what's going on. I expect that a ton of papers will turn up in my post with lots of pencil marks to show me where to sign (I don't expect that I will have the life to read the contracts! Should I? I really ought to, but they're so long!). I expect that the only telephone call I'll get is the one to tell me we've exchanged. I don't expect any communication after the sale except for the bill in the post!

Now the above are my expectations having used legal firms in the past for quite a lot of this sort of thing and you can see that I'm not really expecting any great shakes here. In fact, I'm probably expecting the sort of sausage machine service that I'm likely to get. But this is actually great news as far as my legal practice is concerned; you see they don't really have to do a great deal to exceed my expectations...

Instead of the normal six weeks it takes to process my transaction, my legal firm are going to join up with other legal firms in the area and offer a 'fast track' service that sees the whole thing done, front to back in just four weeks. They're also going to call me once a week just to let me know where we are with the whole process, even if it's just to say that there is no progress. When the contract arrives my solicitor is going to call me and summarise each section for me in plain English, highlighting anything unusual or out of the norm, as well as identifying stuff that's quite standard. When we actually exchange, my legal firm are going to call me to let me know, as well as give me a clear understanding of when we expect to complete. When I get my bill, it will be explained in detail and rounded down so that I end up paying less than I was quoted. Finally, after we have completed my legal firm are going to contact me to ask me for my feedback and if there's anything that I'm not happy about they're going to do something about it.

So take a look at my example above. I think you would agree that if my legal firm behaved in the way I have described above then it's a pretty safe bet that I am actually going to be rather impressed with the service I have received. I hope also that it hasn't escaped your attention that my legal firm haven't needed to invest anything other than their own time to create such a superior experience. These changes needed to exceed the customer experience comes at no physical cost, not a penny, nada, nuffink!

Take note also that there are many changes here to the way my legal firm used to practice. Remember a great customer experience is an amalgam of lots of mini experiences. Some your customers will be consciously aware of some they won't, some of which are beyond your capacity to control yet will nonetheless impact your customers' experience. All of these little mini experiences come together in an underlying sense of positivity (or negativity) that creates advocacy for the legal firm.

In exceeding expectations on so many levels we really do drive the point home that we value the customers' business. We take as many reasonable opportunities as we can to show this and we build a customer experience proposition that will be difficult to follow. More importantly than all of this we will be building our businesses' reputation, ensuring the highest possible level of referrals, as well as capturing the additional opportunities from these existing clients that would have been lost elsewhere to our competitors.

To carry out this exercise for your own business, start by really analysing what your customer experience is (and I bet that this will be different by branch, product or service). Look for those things that you can't control (such as the speed of the solicitor acting for the other party) and think about what you can do to mitigate these eventualities.

Map out in detail the whole customer experience when dealing with your company from the very first moment that the customer makes the decision to use you, and after to the time they get home, and beyond! (Refer back to the exercise we did on the mental mind map earlier in the book if you need help with this). Look carefully for the areas where your customers will have least expectation and consider what you might do to exceed it – don't necessarily think money, think better service! Here's a quick list to get you started:

- What happens when a customer telephones our company?
    - Who answers the telephone?
    - How long does it take for them to answer the telephone?
    - Is that person able to deal with a customer enquiry?
    - What does the customer normally expect from the outcome for their call?
- When customers call into our business what do they expect?
    - Is there any parking? If not where can we guide them to park?
    - How does our business look when people approach?
    - Is it easy to find and well sign posted?
    - Does it give a good 'first impression'?
- Once inside what happens?
    - What does the customer see?
    - Is our business presentable?
    - Who approaches the customer and when?
    - What do we say?
    - Can the customer find what they want easily?
    - Is our business well signposted?

You can see that we have barely touched the surface of this map and we're already asking over a dozen questions about how we manage and exceed our customers' expectations. Take this list and expand on it, making it fit with the type of business you are and the products and services you sell.

You will end up with a list of questions that will challenge the way you look at your business. It's up to you to take action against your list, do the things that are most obviously wrong straight away and work on the others progressively.

Be careful here not to assume that your customers know what your processes are and how long everything takes. I don't move home everyday so how am I to know that the whole process takes two months? When I bring my car in for a service I expect to walk in and leave the keys on the table. How am I to know that you need a quick chat and have some paperwork to complete?

Because these actions are part of your everyday function you know them back to front and inside out, but that doesn't necessarily mean your customers do. You need to manage their expectations by giving them up front information about what's involved and how long it will take. Then you have the opportunity to exceed expectation by delivering your product or service quicker than you had originally indicated.

This is managing expectations and comes from a really good communication ethic that works positively for you. This is an absolute must-have in your business because without good communication you run the risk of falling short of customer expectations.

Taking the team with you

So I've whet your appetite and I hope you're now really enthusiastic about customer service and can't wait to get going – but you can't be everywhere all the time. You will have to engender your team with the values instilled in this book.

This won't always be easy, some of your team will understand what you're trying to achieve and will be really up for it, others won't and will be a challenge but don't let this put you off – you have to do this.

So how can you bring about the change in culture you need to make your business more customer focused? Well, bringing about cultural change takes time and can only be achieved through constant reinforcement of the key messages. Studies have shown that people need to be told something at least 16 times before they really begin to assimilate it. So just walking into your business tomorrow and saying "Right – this is what we're going to do" is unlikely to give you the measurable results you want straightaway.

A lot of your team won't share your enthusiasm and won't see the value in what you're trying to achieve. Many will be too firmly entrenched in their day-to-day routines to see beyond the business processes to the bigger picture and so some radical change is called for. You can't enforce change on your teams thinking – the best you can hope for is that in the long run they'll eventually come around to your way of thinking, but this doesn't help you right now.

What you can do is affect changes to their behaviour.

Your team carry out their day-to-day functions through a prescribed set of behaviours you have specified directly to them. As a boss or business owner you are paying your staff for these behaviours. So what we need to do here is alter and refine these behaviours to be focused on the customer experience – this is something you can do straight away!

You will need to be quite specific here, identifying behaviours and actions that don't meet with your new customer focus and highlighting them to your team. You will need to show them what they're doing wrong and why, and take them from their current position to a new state of behaviours.

So this isn't about choice or way of thinking, it's about what the job entails. Agree with them what changes you want to make and what you expect from them. Remember you're not asking them to change their thinking or attitude – you're requiring them to change their behaviour.

Perhaps the simplest example I can give to explain what I mean came from a throwaway line given to me by a senior manager who was attending a management development workshop we were delivering. We were exploring managing customer expectation and in particular his teams propensity to tell the odd lie now and then to protect themselves from rebuke.

He told a story of an old boss of his who said that there were only ever two lies you could tell: "I'm sorry" and "It's my fault".

This is different thinking and it's a great way to show how you can control behaviour to achieve your objectives. As a manager this guy obviously knew that it wasn't always his fault and I guess there were times when he wasn't particularly sorry. Nevertheless, as a manager this was a function of his job (a set of behaviours he was required to adopt), whether or not he actually agreed with it or believed it was immaterial. It had to be done!

To simplify this even further, in a restaurant it wouldn't be beyond reason to expect the staff to wipe down tables after every sitting because this is a behaviour that they are being paid for. But sure as eggs is eggs, there must be many an occasion where that same member of staff is wiping down a table even though they don't believe that it actually needs it.

But of course the decision of whether or not to wipe down the tables is not theirs. Who's to say that their standards match those of the business? They probably don't, they won't have anywhere near the same degree of ownership. And so to ensure the correct standards and continuity across the business definitive behavioural requirements are implemented, in this case that tables are wiped down after every sitting.

This is no different when it comes to implementing the changes to make your business more customer-focused. You are paying your team to behave in a certain way and that includes how they deal with your customers. There is no choice in this – you're paying them to work this way.

You know I see this all too often and quite a lot in the motor industry, where many of our clients operate. Sales people notoriously determine their own behaviour and this is none more evident than pre-judging customers when they arrive in the showroom.

In a split second they will have assessed a customer's potential to buy a car based on how old they are, what sex they are and how they're dressed. And in that split second they'll make a decision on how much effort, if any, they can be bothered to give this customer.

But this is not only the salesperson's failing, it's the managements too! The salesperson should be equipped with a prescribed set of behaviours that determine exactly how they deal with a customer, a set of behaviours that they should follow with each and every customer, every time. There should be no latitude here to allow the salesperson to decide to what degree they should serve the customer, it's not their choice!

So why does the salesperson behave this way – well mainly because they are allowed too! But also because the salesperson cannot see beyond their day-to-day function of selling cars. They pre-judge their customers because they think that in doing so they can maximise their time more effectively, spending less time on tyre kickers (an unpleasant term used to describe customers that look a lot but don't appear to want to buy) to do other things. Perhaps catching up on paperwork or going for a coffee with colleagues.

Now you and I would know by now that this is narrow thinking. You and I know that there is probably no such thing as a tyre kicker – I mean why would you visit a car dealership if you weren't at least thinking about changing your car at some point in the near future? You and I know that this isn't just about the tangible value of that customer right now in terms of cold hard cash, but also about how they represent our brand to their friends, family and colleagues.

And so when our salesperson can't even be bothered to give these customers the time of day, you and I know that they are slowly poisoning the well of people that are our potential customers.

This is why salespeople should adopt a prescribed, no choice, behaviour towards each and every customer. So that, at the very least, we have prospective customers leaving the business who are saying great things about our attentiveness and attitude, regardless of whether or not they have actually bought anything. This is the beginnings of generating positive word-of-mouth advocacy at street level and is the basis by which your prospective customers will judge you.

Now you and I know this, and you and I understand this but we shouldn't necessarily expect our sales people or staff to know, understand or even care. So we won't allow them to make the decision, choice is removed from the equation.

Make no mistake, behaviours should be demanded (you're paying for them!) and there should be consequences to your team for not behaving in the appropriate manner.

There is no substitution for proper management here and this chapter is intended only to give you an insight into implementing customer focused changes into your business. There are many great management books and advisors out there that can help you if you need it and I urge you to seek them out if you're not absolutely clear on how to make these changes.

Nothing in this book will be of any benefit to you unless you're able to take the learning here and use it to change the way you work in your business.

Managing customer issues – some basics

First off – get in the mindset that customers giving you negative feedback or complaints are good news!

Now that might seem a little strange to you and believe me you're not alone! In fact when I talk to many of my clients about inviting feedback from their customers I'm often met with hesitation and trepidation. In fact it's not unknown for the thought of asking customers for feedback to be rejected altogether by businesses that fear opening the fabled Pandora's box, wary of a torrent of customer negativity. It's almost as if they don't want to see the truth of what's happening. A case of ignorance is bliss!

But understand this, customers giving you negative feedback are giving you two marvellous things!

The first is an invaluable insight into your business and in particular where your business is falling down. Armed with this information you will be able to change the way you look after your customers and really hone the level of service you give them. As we've discussed earlier in this book customer feedback is an excellent road map that tells you the direction in which to take your business.

The second thing customers give you when they raise their displeasures is the opportunity for you to do something about it and for this we should be really grateful!

Why?

Because your customers have to make a positive decision to give you negative feedback and they do so because they're engaged enough with your company to be bothered – let me explain.

Over dinner one evening, the subject turned to customer service (as it quite often does when I'm invited) and I had a very interesting conversation with a gentleman who explained that in restaurants he only ever complained when he liked the owner, the restaurant and the people working there.

If he went somewhere new or was invited as a guest and didn't find the service up to standard or particularly good, he just wouldn't go again. He would pay his bill and leave because they weren't important enough for him to be bothered to tell them that it wasn't good.

In fact, Michael Winner, the famous film director, summed it up nicely – as a renowned and often brutal food critic, Michael described this sort of customer behaviour perfectly. He described a typical evening in a pretty non-descript restaurant where the meal wasn't particularly good. Perhaps the food was cold in places or failed to arrive all at the same time, I'm sure you know exactly what I mean. Nevertheless, when the waiter or waitress arrives at the table and asks if everything is alright we all respond that it is!

Now why do we do this?

Is it because we're not natural complainers? Or because we don't want to offend the waiter/waitress (after all it wasn't their fault the food was cold). Or is it that we just can't be bothered with all the fuss?

The truth is that years of evolutionary development have made us wary of conflict, when we're asked if everything is OK, we only really have two answers – yes or no. The latter of these two invariably requires further interaction and possibly even conflict should our waiter disagree. And then, as we have discovered, it's highly likely that we're simply not engaged enough to make the effort to say how bad it is.

Not that it would matter because your waiter/waitress probably doesn't have the necessary skills to deal with your complaints even if you made the effort to make them. Let me tell you about a personal experience that illustrates this.

An Easter half term break found my family and I at a pub-diner called The Hoops Inn somewhere between Bideford and Barnstable. Now The Hoops Inn is a fairly innocuous thatched pub that is trying to set itself above the rest by elevating the standard of food and charging restaurant prices. Now that's OK, I don't have a problem with anyone wanting to do better and be better but I do have a problem when the standard to the food and service doesn't match the price.

I have to be honest and say that I wasn't in the best of moods – I hadn't wanted a restaurant meal and was in the mood for fish and chips but we didn't know the area and the kids were hungry, so in the absence of anything else, this was it.

The food was poor and certainly not worth the money we were charged for it. My sausage and mash was mediocre to say the least and certainly not restaurant standard. Yet for the money I paid for it I could have fed all five of us with it if I had bought and cooked it myself. The kids' pasta was worse, a horrible glutinous mess that was hideously expensive for what it was, even at kids' menu prices. So you get the picture, it wasn't good! We ate up quickly and made our way out as soon as we could.

I waited at the bar to settle the bill, while my wife and kids made their way back to the car. As the barmaid processed my credit card she asked the usual insincere question: "Was everything alright for you?" Expecting me to reply in just the way I have explained above, this time, however, she was in for a surprise.

"No," I replied: "The food was actually lousy and nowhere near worth the money you're charging me for it."

"Oh," she said. Then she handed back my card and gave me my receipt and that was that! No offer of an apology, no enquiry as to why I was so unhappy. She just gave me my card and turned to serve another customer!

And this level of ineptitude isn't just reserved for country pubs. It exists even in more exclusive establishments such as the Charing Cross Hotel in the centre of London opposite the Strand. I was invited to lunch by a very professional and talented lady by the name of Helen Cambell Watt who works for Coutts Bank in the heart of London. The reception we had at the Charing Cross Hotel wasn't particularly helpful but this seemed to be compensated by the wonderfully looking appetising food served up for us. Delightful and tasty indeed, had the hand cut chips been cooked properly.

Our waiter arrived to take away the dishes and settle our bill and asked if everything was OK. To highlight a point I had been discussing with Helen during the meal I said that it was not. I explained that the chips were not cooked and therefore inedible. The waiter laughed a nervous laugh as if I were pulling his leg, which meant that I had to spell out my dissatisfaction in detail so that he could see that I was not. His reaction was exactly the same! Without any further discussion or interaction he took the money, turned heel and left!

Now I could have taken the opportunity to kick up a right fuss and demanded to see the manager or my money back but do you know what, I just couldn't be bothered.

I mean what was the point?

What was I going to achieve?

In reality, nothing!

I had absolutely no intention of ever visiting them again and would make a point of warning away my friends, family, business colleagues (and you). I had about as much desire in seeing them improve as they had of making sure I was happy!

And why? Well, even though I gave them every opportunity to put things right, they didn't. They didn't put them right because they didn't have the skills to deal with a disgruntled customer and because they lacked these skills, they lost a customer.

"No great shakes" – you may say. After all I was only a passing guest, it's not as if I was a local or a regular, they haven't really lost out have they?

Well, yeah they have.

They missed out on an opportunity to learn how to improve their service, the quality of their food and the skills of their staff. They missed out on invaluable feedback that would have given them a really good steer on how to make themselves stand out among their competition. Instead they will carry doing what they do, ignorantly thinking they're doing a great job when in fact they are mediocre at best.

For some of them their repeat business will be poor, but they won't notice because they won't know any different. Their reputation will do nothing to drive their business forward and they will wonder why their marketing doesn't deliver the results they had hoped for. In the end they will blame the recession for their woes and if they're really lucky they might survive, but it will always be a struggle – all for the lack of some genuine interest in the customer's experience.

This is why it's absolutely essential that we pay attention to our customers and look for reasons why it might not have been as good as it should. It's why we should look for good constructive criticism and see it for what it is – sound advice to make our business better. But fundamentally it's why we should learn how to deal with customer negativity so that we can make it work for us, not only to provide us with good quality learning but also to help convert a disillusioned customer into a customer for life!

So you can see that in the main it's a positive decision on the part of the customer to give you negative feedback but it doesn't always work this way. Some customers have no choice other than to complain.

If having bought a new washing machine it goes wrong within the first few weeks of ownership I'm going to be miffed. But I'm also going to be without a washing machine and that's going to seriously inconvenience me. So I'm annoyed (it's totally unacceptable that my washing machine has only lasted a couple of weeks) and I want it put right.

I make a call to the retailer, not because I want them to benefit from my feedback but because I want my washing machine fixed.

Maybe, if I was a multi-millionaire and just plain stupid with my money, I might just throw this one away and go and buy another. The retailer would never know that anything was wrong – except for one thing, they wouldn't be benefitting from my replacement purchase.

So there are times when customers complain because they have to.

But none of this actually matters because the point of real importance here is the fact that you have the opportunity to put things right. If you act quickly and professionally you will take a customer through the positive loop of affirmation that we spoke about earlier in this book and just maybe create this fabled customer for life!

Now, unhappy customers by their very nature can be difficult to deal with if you don't know how. There are a definite set of skills you and your team should adopt to manage customers that have a serious grievance. I'm going to give you some basic skills in the next chapter that will help you get to the bottom of a problem and work to resolving issues positively and professionally.

The Customer Complaints Iceberg

Earlier on in this book we looked at the sphere of influence any one of us has as a prospective customer on the reputation of a business. We showed that a poor customer experience impacts on our business reputation through word-of-mouth and that our reputation is influenced even by those individuals that are not customers.

The customer complaints iceberg takes this a step further and examines the negative impact of complaints in your business. Here it is below:

The Customer Complaints Iceberg

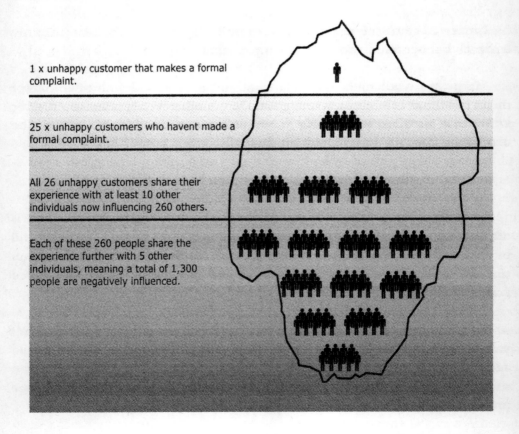

1 x unhappy customer that makes a formal complaint.

25 x unhappy customers who havent made a formal complaint.

All 26 unhappy customers share their experience with at least 10 other individuals now influencing 260 others.

Each of these 260 people share the experience further with 5 other individuals, meaning a total of 1,300 people are negatively influenced.

Now it's important that you fully understand the impact of the customer complaints iceberg. What it tells us is that for every complaint we receive there is a hugely broader and more significant impact on our business reputation. What this means is that when we receive a complaint we can be pretty sure that this isn't an isolated incident and that a good number of customers have had a similar experience, but couldn't be bothered to complain about it.

The circumstances that occurred to cause this complaint have in all likelihood happened before and will happen again, unless we take action to prevent this.

Now most businesses have a blinkered view to complaints. For starters they don't appreciate the wider impact of the complaint on their business. The better ones will focus on dealing with the specific issues raised by the specific customer and work to resolve them in a way that creates a positive advocate. We've talked a lot about this earlier in the book.

Problem is that this is just half the job!

Sure we've dealt with customer issues, we've turned a detractor into a promoter and will benefit from all that entails, but this is just the tip of the iceberg. What about all of those other customers that got the same negative experience but didn't bother to complain? Well, it's unlikely we can do anything about their individual experience if they're not prepared to share it with us? But that doesn't mean that we shouldn't take steps to prevent the problems happening again. After all prevention is better than cure.

Every complaint we receive is a massive sign post that there is something seriously wrong in our business. The skill for us is to recognise that this problem probably goes beyond just this one complaint and we need to take steps to root out and correct the circumstances that caused it once and for all.

Of course this supports what I have always said, in so much that complaints shouldn't be considered to be a bad thing, moreover as a steer towards the weaker areas of our business that need our attention.

Look carefully at the customer's complaint, really get to understand what happened and why? Look at your processes and work out what you can do to ensure that you don't get a repeat of the problem. Now this is a lot more work than just dealing with a single customer complaint but if you truly want to deliver a great customer experience its essential for your long-term success. Not only that, it will propel you streets ahead of your competitors who will continue to spend valuable amounts of time, effort and cash dealing with complaints, rather than building great customer experiences.

And this brings me nicely to my final point about dealing with complaints. For me businesses fall into one of two categories when it comes to handling complaints:

- Mitigating exposure
  or
- Investing in advocacy.

Many companies are geared specifically towards mitigation when it comes to complaints. They are looking for ways to minimise the financial impact of the complaint on their business. Quite often these businesses will reject a complaint or just generally make things difficult. They will give the impression that they mistrust you and refuse to accept responsibility perhaps even suggesting that you are somehow at fault. My bet is that most of you have experienced just this sort of thing.

This approach is fundamentally flawed for a whole host of reasons. It makes no provision for the whole life value of the customer, nor does it consider the negative impact of such behaviour on the business' reputation through word-of-mouth. In fact, in my opinion it's a disastrous policy that will unquestionably have an effect on the businesses long-term profitability.

On the other hand there are companies, such as Apple that have a different approach to customer issues, seeing them as opportunities to build advocacy and reputation. Notice that I used the words customer issues rather than customer complaints when talking about companies such as Apple. This is because a complaint is normally a manifestation of an issue that hasn't been properly addressed. Businesses that are focused on the customer experience seldom have complaints, choosing instead to deal effectively with customer issues as they arise.

And when presented with customer issues, rather than arguing the toss in an attempt to reduce their financial exposure, they work hard to take the customer through the positive loop of affirmation in order to create a relationship that makes them a customer for life. If you refer back to the section earlier in the book on the Positive Loop of Affirmation, you will remember that it's not enough just to put things right, if you want to keep your customer for life then you have to show them that you really value their business and go the extra step/mile to show this.

I started by using Apple as a reference point and there was a specific reason for this. Apart from the fact that I believe it to be one of the most customer focused businesses I have come across and that's not just my opinion. In fact most of the people I know that have been in our local Apple store would agree, especially my chum Jonathan Warren who uses the Apple iPhone for everyone in his sign business. He described his visit to the Apple store in Cabot Circus in Bristol to me and to everyone else by the sound of it.

He was having a few minor problems with his telephone and called into the store to see if they could help him get it sorted. He knew he was just out of warranty and fully expected at the very least to pay for a repair or even perhaps a new replacement.

As I would expect, the team in the store were very attentive and couldn't do enough to welcome him and arrange for him to see a specialist. He didn't have to wait too long, but while he did he was given an iPad to keep him entertained. After a few minutes he was called forward and explained to the assistant who he was and the problems he was having with his telephone. Even though the assistant agreed with him that his telephone was just out of warranty, he commented that this problem wasn't the sort of thing he would expect of an iPhone and promptly replaced it with a brand new one free of charge!

Now – what's the thinking behind this? Surely it can't be commercial to replace everyone's telephone out of warranty?

What's happening here is that the sales assistant has been empowered to take a balanced view on the legitimacy of problems his customers encounter and rather than looking to mitigate his company's exposure he looks to invest in positive advocacy. Now it can't be by accident that Apple has an enviable customer advocacy that borders on fanaticism, it's clear to me that they develop their reputation by investing in advocacy. My friend Jonathan isn't expecting anything other than a costly repair or worse still the cost of a replacement. He certainly isn't expecting to be given a telephone there and then completely free of charge. So what has Apple actually achieved here.

Well for starters, Jonathan will never buy any other telephone and if he wasn't an Apple nut before he probably is now. So our amiable assistant has probably guaranteed a good proportion of this customer's whole life value, wonder what that equates to? For certain it won't be insignificant.

Added to that of course is another voice exalting the Apple brand and re-endorsing a reputation for outstanding customer service. Jonathan is quite happy to sing the praises of Apple whenever the opportunity arises, so apple's investment in advocacy seems certainly to be paying off, if just in terms of positive advertising from a happy customer.

Then of course there are more than one or two mentions of Apple in this book. None of which I stress are the consequence of anything other than a positive experience.

So, the investment in advocacy, has it paid off? I think I would say so!

Managing customers in difficult circumstances

Most businesses I know engage their staff in some form of training or other. Many spend vast fortunes on giving the extensive product knowledge or really intensive sales skills, but rarely do I find a company that gives its staff the sort of skills they need to manage a customer when things go wrong.

Quite often the consequence of this is that the situation often becomes exacerbated through poor customer service skills and just goes from bad to worse. It need not be this way if we just learnt a few simple rules to help us deal with these circumstances.

Dealing with a customer that is upset

First off I'm going to tell you what to do when you've got an angry customer to deal with.

I'm going to start with something that you should never, ever tolerate. Customers that are upset (many of whom have a genuine grievance) are often referred to in derogatory terms. Labelled as nutters or screamers these individuals are converted from paying customers to low-life non-entities in an instance. And this sets the scene for anyone dealing with this customer from then on. It's a chain of prejudice that has separated the individual away from being a customer to becoming a nuisance and it's wrong!

Never, never, ever allow your staff to say anything remotely derogatory about any of your customers. It's an absolute cardinal sin and if you catch them doing it, pick them up on it straight away. Here's a little saying for you.

A customer is not always right but they are always the customer!

This says that as a very minimum we should treat the customer with professional courtesy at all times. We don't have to agree with them, we don't even have to believe them but we must always treat them with courtesy and respect. They are after all our customer and without customers none of us would have jobs. It also says that customers do make mistakes but that doesn't mean that they are any the less important to us.

So we accept that our customers may, every now and then, have the right to

131

be upset with us, particularly if we've done something wrong. And we accept that it is their right to be treated with a certain level of respect and professionalism. Holding our customers in such high regard will ensure that we have the opportunity to repair even difficult circumstances.

Firstly, take on board this critical piece of information, a customer that is really upset and sounding off is not doing so because of a single incident. In fact there will have been a succession of incidents and ineptitudes that have accumulated and culminated in one very aggrieved customer. It's important that you know this because it will help you understand that the customer has reached the end of their tether. They want you to understand how disappointed they are and it maybe that they feel an expression of anger is the only way in which you will take them seriously.

Ultimately, when you are dealing with a customer that's upset there are two key things you must do to placate the situation:

1. Give them your name and your direct contact number, take responsibility
2. Tell them how you're going to deal with the issues and when you will be speaking with them next.

Most customers will expect a complete lack of responsibility and ownership of their problem, in fact this could be a contributing factor to their frustrations. Taking ownership of the problem can be achieved by giving the customer as much detail as you can about who you are and how they can contact you, using direct numbers rather than a switchboard.

This will give the customer a genuine sense that you will deal with their problem rather than just pass it off to the next shift of customer service advisors.

Now that the customer knows who you are, the next thing is to let them know what you're going to do and when. A customer won't necessarily expect you to resolve the problem there and then, and this will of course depend on the circumstances, but if you need to do some investigation tell your customer this, tell them how long this will take and tell them when you will call them next.

This is about managing their expectations and a structured plan of resolution will give them a sense that their problems are being taken seriously and are actually being attended to. One word of caution here, do not set deadlines that you cannot meet and make sure that you always contact the customer when you say you will. If you don't be prepared for a whole heap of trouble to come down on you!

The next thing we must take on board is that a customer who is really upset (and not being backward about showing it) is showing their frustration at their particular circumstances not at us as individuals, we should never take it personally. It's too easy to see customer criticism as being levelled at us personally, which it almost never is.

If you can detach yourself personally from such criticism you have a much better chance of looking at the problem objectively, this will help you get to the real issues and formulate a strategy to put things right.

Being personally detached doesn't mean that you shouldn't empathise with your customers circumstances, in fact it's essential that you do. Use phrases like "I can understand how you feel" and "you must be very disappointed" to show that you can relate to their position.

Start by allowing your customer the courtesy of sounding off without being interrupted. Quite often customers have to be driven to make complaints and it's normally after a chain of events that have progressively exacerbated the situation. So, by the time they get to you they're probably quite upset and need to get their angst off their chest, let them, it's better for you both if you do.

There's a knack to this, you have to show your customer that even though they're sounding off at you that you're listening and taking in what they're saying. You can do this with simple acknowledgements such as "I understand", "uh huh", "I see", "of course" and so on, you get the picture.

What you mustn't do – never, ever – is interrupt or argue, wait for your turn. Your customer will let you know when they're ready for your response.

You'll know when you get this right because your customer will normally say something like "I'm sorry to have a go at you, I know it's not your fault but I'm very upset about what's happened" and when you get this you know that you have successfully let the storm blow out.

OK – so now we have a customer who already feels better about sounding off at you but we still have to deal with the issues that brought us here. Now I expect that somewhere along the line we've done something wrong, maybe even a few things – if that's the case explain the situation and/or admit the mistakes. If it's your companies fault don't make excuses, fess up and apologise.

Don't get stuffy here, it's not you as an individual that's apologising, it's you as your company's representative. Remember this isn't about you, so apologising should never be an issue and it won't be if you don't take the criticism personally.

Offer your customer some alternatives to put things right and allow them to choose what works best for them, remember if your company's in the wrong then you should be the ones putting yourselves out to put them right again. We shouldn't be inconveniencing the customer any further if we can possibly help it.

A friend of mine owns and runs a restaurant and was telling me about a particularly difficult and embarrassing moment he had with a customer. He openly admitted that his team had dropped the ball and that his poor customer had undergone a series of calamities one after another, and that they were quite understandably not at all happy.

He started by telling me that he had given them their wine for free but that as things got worse he ended up telling his customer that of course they wouldn't have to pay for the meal as he apologised profusely.

"What more could I have done?" he asked.

The problem is, as I pointed out to him, that you haven't really done anything. If I had had the same experience myself I would have refused to pay the bill, so offering it to me on the house had no value to me. If he really wanted to make amends and show the customer that he valued her business then he needed to go the extra mile to show it.

If it were me I would have said something along the following lines:

"I am deeply sorry that you have had such a terrible experience with us here this evening and I expect that you are extremely disappointed. This is not the level of service we expect for our customers and this sort of thing barely ever happens.

"Of course we won't be charging you for anything this evening and with your permission I would like to invite you all back again, at your convenience, where I would like to show you that we can give you a fabulous evening – and I won't be charging you for that either!"

Fixing things just isn't enough if you want to take the customer through the positive loop of affirmation. In this instance not charging for a really poor meal is what I would expect as a customer so you have to go beyond that and give the customer something they wouldn't expect if you want to win them back. You have to show the customer that you really do value their custom.

So in summary:

- Let the storm blow out:
  - Wait until the customer has finished being angry
  - Never interrupt
  - Never argue
  - Acknowledge you're listening
- Empathise:
  - "I can understand how you feel"
  - "You must be very disappointed"
- Explain the situation but don't make excuses
- Offer an alternative positive solution to put it right
- Remember – the customer isn't mad at you personally, they're upset about the circumstances.

What to do when things go wrong

We can often avoid having to deal with upset customers by being better at managing problems when they arise, rather than allowing them to accumulate to the point where the customer has had enough.

Managing such problems often involves us having to have a difficult conversation with the customer, which is likely to disappoint them. As a consequence staff often shy away from dealing directly with these problems sometimes to the extent where they even kid themselves that it will all be alright in the end.

Arming yourselves with the right skills can go a long way to building your self-confidence in your ability to handle these difficult circumstances. Here are a few tips that can help:

First off deliver bad news straight away

Nobody wants to hear bad news but your customers will appreciate the opportunity to plan accordingly, which they won't get if you leave it to the last moment before you tell them.

Speak only to the customer, don't cop out

Giving bad news isn't easy and something we would all rather avoid but your customers will appreciate your personal contact. Don't cop out by leaving voicemails.

Empathise with your customer

Use phrases such as "you must be really disappointed", "I'm sure it's a dreadful inconvenience" to show you share your customers concerns.

Explain the situation but don't make excuses

Absolutely do not lie, you will get caught out. Explain the problem and confess if it's your fault, use phrases like "the reason we haven't fixed your product is because we didn't order the parts as we should have".

Offer an alternative solution to put things right

"Customer we can either keep your product here for a few more days and fix it when the parts arrive or we can return it to you and collect it again?"

Of course if we looked after our customers properly, did things we were supposed to do when we were supposed to do them, took care to ensure that our customers experience was a positive one at every step of the way, it's unlikely that we will have a customer that would be so unhappy. Can't think of anywhere that fits this description though.

Managing staff – one agenda

This section is particularly important for those businesses with remote management/staff who work together in small numbers or are prone to periodic quiet spells, often without supervision.

It is particularly relevant to the customer experience as staff that are subjected to extended periods of inactivity find themselves stupefied. This is because staff that are allowed to do nothing quite often do just that and this in turn quickly finds them in a catatonic state brought about by inactivity – how do I know this? Well it happened to me.

Many years ago one of my very first jobs as a young man involved working for a retail company selling goods for motorists. I joined the company after a recent acquisition that saw it with far more shops than staff to manage them.

I had worked with the company for only a few months before I found myself running one of the quieter stores on the outskirts of Bristol, I was the manager and the only member of staff.

The nature of the store was such that during the week customers were few and far between and so I often found myself sitting at the counter reading a paper or chatting on the telephone, in fact pretty much anything that involved breaking up the day – let's just say that my "back in five mins" sign had plenty of wear.

Now I was just a young fella but I should have known better. I was being paid (albeit not very much) to manage the store, when in reality I did very little but this wasn't only my fault, my superiors should have managed me better and I will tell you why.

Inactivity inevitably leads to boredom, which is exacerbated by the fact that these individuals are to all intents and purposes incarcerated within the confines of the building, unable to leave if just to alleviate the tedium. The end result is a slow and inevitable physical and mental shut down, descent into a catatonic stupor is not uncommon and difficult to break free from and I would imagine that you have all experienced these effects of which daydreaming is one of them.

Some individuals seek relief from boredom through extensive conversation with others or in other ways; the proliferation of smart phones presents many individuals with a whole bag of things to keep them amiably entertained without having to move from the spot. These activities or inactivities have no association with the business, they are separate from work tasks and have their own agendas and objectives that need to be fulfilled. Let me expand.

Sadly it is not uncommon to find oneself in a retail outlet where the staff are too busily engaged in personal conversations to be properly attentive to their customers. It's a big irritation for me. I feel like I have no importance to these staff who would clearly much prefer it if I just left and allowed them to carry on with their conversation – I have become an interruption to what they're doing!

Now we spoke about this earlier in the book where processes can wrongly become the focus and misguided individuals feel the need to put process above dealing with customers. This is very similar but the gap created by a lack of any work to do has been filled by personal objectives, everything else becomes secondary and that includes seeing to the needs of customers.

In my experience there is in fact plenty to do it's just that the staff would much rather be involved in conversation, gossip, reading the paper or chatting on Facebook, wouldn't we all! So inactivity shows poor management and poor management processes. Lack of direction and guidance allows staff to make their own decisions about what and what they're not going to do and the consequences for your business can be catastrophic!

I have watched customers walk into a shop who are clearly minded to buy but leave quickly because the environment wasn't conducive to buy. In fact many of these stores sell goods in spite of themselves.

Why do your staff behave this way? Because you let them!

Look, I know that you can't be everywhere all of the time and I know that your staff are never going to have the same focus on customer service as you do but that doesn't mean that we can't manage them better. This is essential if we are to create an engaging environment for our customers, this is all about creating the right focus.

If your staff think it's OK for anything to take precedence over serving the customer then that's because you haven't made it clear to the contrary. You can't necessarily expect your staff to have the same customer service philosophy as you do but that's ok because you can expect them to behave in a certain way because that's what they are paid to do!

Tell me where it says in your staff employment contract that they can pick and choose which customers to serve and can ignore others if they wish – it doesn't, so why let them behave this way?

Avoid lethargy at all costs, it really is the breeding ground for this sort of behaviour. Develop a formatted structure of the basic level of presentation for your business and make sure that it is your staff's responsibility to maintain this level – above all measure it. Make sure your team know that nothing is more important than serving the customer and that everything else comes second.

Then manage.

If business is slow, it will show in your earnings and you should therefore expect your staff with more time on their hands to keep the presentation of your business tip top. Conversely, if it's clear you've been busy, cut them some slack but make sure they're clear on what they have to do the next quiet moment they get. Keep your people busy, in the end it will make the day go faster and keep their focus up.

Good customer service makes commercial sense

The fact of the matter is that good customer service makes good commercial sense and I can prove it.

Using real data from one of my very first and most long-standing clients we conducted a research exercise to establish how customer service impacted on a customer's sense of value for money.

Using a sample of 1,000 customers we asked those who had enjoyed a great customer experience to tell us to what degree they saw value for money and more than 97% of them felt that they had good or OK value for money. Conversely when we asked the same question to those customers that had a bad experience more than 75% of them felt that there was little or no value for money whatsoever.

Now perhaps that is not so surprising, after all one might expect happy customers to see value for money and unhappy customers to not – but this is kind of missing the point.

You see in principle there is very little difference in the circumstances between them, all the data, and therefore our sample, came from the same company. This meant that all the customers had visited the same premises, they were all quoted the same prices, they were served by the same staff, they bought the same products and services. In fact everything relating to the purchase was exactly the same for them all, the only difference between them was the experience they had!

So what does this tell us? Well quite simply if you want more than 97% of your customers to believe that they get good value for money from your business then you need to give them all a great customer experience.

Take this a step further if you feel that your business is under pressure to compete on price. I've said it before and I will say it again, there is no such thing as expensive! Only a poor sense of value for the products or services provided. If we only ever bought on price then we would all be driving small cheap cars and nobody would ever buy a premium product or brand.

Let's explore this further and look at Harrods, for me the world's most reconised retail brand. For those of you that have visited Harrods you will know that they are all about the customer experience and that they are not cheap. What you might not know is that Harrods has an established tradition of supplying its customers with whatever they want, absolutely anything!

In days of yore it was quite possible to ask Harrods for an elephant and fully expect them to supply one. Of course the trade in endangered animals means that today such a thing would be unthinkable and not at all good for their public image, nonetheless the spirit of this undertaking should not be lost. No doubt one would pay excessively for anything out of the ordinary or not normally stocked, but the point here is that the level of service you can expect from Harrods knows no bounds, provided of course that you are prepared to pay for it. Then again, where would you start looking if you wanted to buy an elephant! And this is exactly the point, price isn't always the issue, it's what you get overall for the price you pay that's important.

So think about what you offer your customers against what you're charging them. Think about the experience they get from you for the price that they pay and compare it to your competitors. If you feel that your competitor gives a better pound for pound experience than you do, then your customers will see you as expensive and not good value for money.

The good news here is that you don't have to compete just on price! If you want to protect your margins, focus on giving a great customer experience, so much so that price barely factors into the equation. There's plenty to refer to in this book that will help you achieve this but in essence you're looking to exceed expectation and this does not need to be at all costly.

So we've seen here how a great customer experience makes good commercial sense and I guess that it's therefore pretty obvious that a bad experience will have the opposite effect – straightforward enough. However the commercialism of a negative customer experience isn't just reflected by the negative effects of losing a customer and the ensuing bad publicity that will generate but also to physical costs of dealing with a customer complaint itself.

Counting the cost of poor customer service can be more obvious than it seems especially when you consider the lifetime value of your customer, a simple fact lost on even some of our largest, best-known corporate brands.

I'm going to tell you about and experience we have had with one of the big four supermarket chains – Morrisons.

We've already discussed how big corporates can lose sight of individual customer experiences, even perhaps become blasé, after all what's the loss of one customer in the grand scale of things? This we know is flawed thinking, particularly for bigger corporates whose customer reputation is the accumulative sum of countless individual customer experiences.

It's flawed because it makes premise that losing one customer to poor customer service is unlikely to make an impact to the business because it assumes that only one customer has experienced poor service. In fact the converse is true the mere fact that one customer is lost exposes an inadequate customer service process that has failed. The argument is that if it has failed once then it will undoubtedly fail again and, given the scale of customers big corporates experience, the scale of failure can be truly monumental indeed. This ultimately is loss of market share and it happens all the time.

Like many supermarkets Morrisons have ventured beyond just food sales to include many other additional services and in particular a full dry cleaning service available at our local store, where my wife takes all our household dry-cleaning (which is by no means a meagre amount with three kids and two wardrobes full of suits).

On this particular occasion my wife had deposited a rather impressive jumpsuit, which she had borrowed from a friend to attend a 1970s disco fancy dress party. It was festooned by iridescent patches of reflective silver that shone the many colours of the rainbow as they caught the light, the sort of thing you would only ever wear at such a party.

Being quite a conscientious person my wife thought that it was only right and proper to get the garment cleaned before returning it to her friend and took it into Morrisons, who checked it in and gave her a receipt. So far so good.

Unfortunately, when she came to collect the garment all was not well. The patches of silver material that made the suit what it was had tarnished in much the same way as a silver spoon might when left to oxidise in the open air over extended periods of time. In effect it was trashed.

You can imagine that my wife was not best pleased and the assistant that served here was not exactly helpful. In the end we were told that it would have to be referred to the regional manager to make a decision.

Make a decision! What decision was there to make?! Let me help you here, we gave you the garment perfect in every way (well maybe a bit smelly) and you gave it back fit only for washing the dishes. There's no decision here, let's talk about what you're going to do to put it right! If only...

No, like it or not due process was going to be served. Never let it be said that Morrisons will put customer service in the way of a perfectly good process (hmmm – seems to be a bit of a picture emerging here of supermarkets and their processes).

Sadly for us, the due process seemed to take an inordinate amount of time and after the passing of several weeks and several unreturned telephone calls (and that is a whole other story) we eventually receive a letter, yes a letter.

So, first off what does a letter mean? What does it translate into when we think of customer service? I will tell you.

A letter means several things:

- I cannot be bothered to speak with you directly
- I am scared that you might give me a hard time if I call you
- You can't give me a hard time if I write to you, so nah!
- I'm not confident that my argument holds up
- I'm being very formal
- I am following a process

Now, being formal and following a process are sometimes very necessary but only after you have spoken with the customer, otherwise a letter is just a cop out. Let's not forget that customers aren't stupid and will recognise it for what it is.

My letter very formally advises me that it wasn't their fault that they destroyed the garment, it was the garment manufacturers fault! You see the garment manufacturer gave dry cleaning instructions on the care label that were obviously wrong because when followed the end result was oblivion for the poor old 1970s jumpsuit. If my wife wanted compensation I should take it up with the manufacturer.

Enter me.

So, I found myself on the telephone with some nameless and faceless individual who let me talk for some minutes about the problem before informing me that he would get someone to call me back. "No, no, no," I said, "that just won't do. We have had countless promises of a call back that have never materialised, I would like to speak with someone that can actually make a decision now! Please."

So I get put through to a lady called Dawn and I go through the whole story again and Dawn informs me that it wasn't their fault, they had merely followed the instructions on the label.

"I'm really sorry" I said, "but your argument doesn't stand up."

"After all," I explained, "if the care label said please boil for 40 minutes on a high heat with two onions and a carrot, would you do it?"

And of course the answer is no, because with some degree of dry cleaning knowledge it would be pretty obvious that this wouldn't do the garment any good at all – and here is the argument. I expect a company like Morrisons to have some degree of expertise when handling dry cleaning goods. I expect them to recognise a suspect or difficult garment when they see one and I expect them to either reject the garment as un-cleanable or perhaps test it on an inconspicuous area just to be sure.

But do you know what? This isn't really the point of this example. There's something much worse going on here, an underlying level of incompetency that is worse than the pathetic excuses for the incompetent dry cleaning service. It's the total lack of consideration for the customer experience and the complete ignorance of the wider cost of this incompetence. Let me explain to you as I did to Dawn.

You see what Dawn forgot, or didn't know about or plain just didn't care about was how this whole experience was making me feel. Neither did she give a moment's thought to the impact of this negative experience, not just on me, a regular loyal customer, but on everybody that I come into contact with, with whom I share this story (the many of you that are reading this for example).

Worse still, as I explained to Dawn, their pointless, defensive reaction to this

145

unfortunate event had probably already cost them more in person hours on the telephone and in impersonal letters than it would have if they had just compensated me with a replacement. And this is the stupidity of it all.

Any sensible business with a good customer focus would have reacted completely differently. Rather than argue the toss a sensible business would have compensated the customer AND given them 50% off of their next dry cleaning bill. A sensible business would know that in the long-run this would be the cheapest way of resolving the issue and the most likely way of guaranteeing their continued custom.

Furthermore, a sensible business would know that I would be impressed (and perhaps relieved) in how customer focused they were and that I was very likely to recommend them to my friends and family. And in the long-run a sensible business would recognise that this would be better for them than squirming out of a situation that they should have given the customer the benefit of the doubt in the first place.

So, what exactly has this episode cost Morrisons?

Well for starters I think it's safe to say that I will not be returning to Morrisons to have my dry cleaning done, by my calculations that probably amounts to at least £500 a year and we have been using them for the past five years so if we used them for the next five years that would be at least £2,500.

Added to that is the foolish waste of time taken by the handful of individuals that we have spoken with and have sent us letters and I have no doubt in real terms we are probably looking easily at £200 – £300.

Then of course there are all of you out there reading this that are questioning whether Morrisons is the sort of company you want to deal with and I am sure that there at least few of you that will be influenced by my experience and will avoid (consciously or unconsciously) using Morrisons at the very least for dry cleaning. Not forgetting of course all of my close friends colleagues and family who are already completely switched off from Morrisons. What price can I put on this? I'm not sure but I do know that it will not be insignificant.

And so you can see yet again how processes distract from the most important factor for any business – the customer experience. I hope now that you can also start to equate the cost of this distraction to your business. Anything other than a complete focus on your customer experience is a false economy and will cost you dear – one way or the other!

The rubbish service I got from Dawn and her team meant that once again she failed to call me back as promised and so not to be outdone I contacted Morrisons head office, where the lady on the telephone switchboard tried to re-connect me to the customer service team. "No, no," I said, "I don't want to speak with them because they're rubbish, I want to speak with a director of your company because I think they would be astounded if they knew how poor your customer service team are!"

And so, after much fuss, I eventually get to speak with Janice, who is the PA to the Chairman of Morrisons (whose name I forget) and I explain to her who I am and why I'm calling and in particular how inadequate their customer service team are. "Of course," I said "if you seriously want to compete with the other big three supermarkets, customer service will be a key battleground for you".

Janice listened politely, although I never really thought she got it, and said that she needed to investigate and come back to me – guess what?

Cardinal sin, she abdicated responsibility to the customer service team (you know the inept rubbish one) and a week or so later we received a letter from them still denying all responsibility but offering £20 of Morrisons' vouchers because we said we had bad service.

"We said we had bad service!"

Not "We're sorry we didn't look after you properly" but "we said we had bad service!" The ineptitude compounds itself! Morrisons – I do hope you're reading this because you really suck at customer service.

You know the cost of this ridiculous attempt to mitigate the complaint is not the only financial consideration here, what about the whole lifetime value of a customer?

The whole lifetime value of your customer is the potential income you could see from this customer assuming their continued ongoing custom. This will vary for many of you and is dependent on the goods or services you sell. Many products have a typical lifespan, cars and upholstery, for example, are typically changed on a three year cycle. So when you calculate the whole lifetime value of your customer you need to consider how much of your product or service customers would reasonably be expected to purchase during their lifetime. Their lifetime being the time you would expect them to continue to buy from you.

For those of you that run your own businesses, think about your exit strategy, when you plan to sell up or retire and use that as your timescale – this will be a direct reflection of the value of a customer to you.

So let's think this through, what do we need to consider?

- The number of times our customer could reasonably be expected to make a purchase during our timescale
- The average value of that purchase
- The profit we make on that purchase
- The other, secondary purchases we might expect our customers to buy (extra services or up- sold products)

Then there's:

- The number of customers they introduce to our business that we can reasonably expect to stay with us for the duration of our timescale.

When we start to add all of this up it's not hard to see that, including the recommendations we get from our customers that the whole lifetime value can be incredibly significant, even if you're a low ticket business that relies on volume.

I wonder exactly what my lifetime value could have been with Morrisions? It is probably quite considerable, which makes its handling of our situation all the more ridiculous.

I want to put a caveat on all of the above, mainly because there are a few unscrupulous individuals out there who look for every opportunity to make a gain at the expense of others including you and your business.

You see the essence of the supplier/customer relationship is one of an exchange of value. In exchange for goods or services there is an explicit understanding of cost and the needs of the supplier to make a profit. So when an individual seeks to gain goods or services at the expense of the suppliers profitability they are operating outside of the essence of this relationship and therefore in my opinion they forfeit any right to be called a customer.

Now that we understand that these people are nothing short of crooks we can remove the label of customer and allow ourselves the opportunity to deal with them in a completely different manner. We no longer need to consider any of the things we have so carefully covered in this book – we need only concern ourselves on how quickly we can remove them from our premises forever. You will always have the right to choose not to have someone as a customer, the right to tell someone to shop elsewhere and that you do not want their custom. But only if they transcend the sacred supplier/customer relationship. Be very careful not to tar everyone with the same brush and don't suspect everyone of trying to con you. Be conscious that most of your customers will have a genuine grievance. Start on that basis and you should be ok. As far as those unscrupulous individuals are concerned, give them short shrift.

Customer service and social media

Firstly, don't let the rise of all things social media scare you!

To start with you need to understand that the basis of all social media revolves around one central maxim as described by a clever chap at our PR company: "Social media is nothing more than content created by its audience." Once we understand this we can begin to understand how to work with it.

The most common social media used today are Facebook and Twitter but there are many other forms of social media that comprise of forums, ratings sites and collectives of individuals with a common underlying interest. Essentially they all operate with the same basic function, they allow the user to express themselves through comment. Such comment is extensive in nature and topic and is generally formed from basic emotional content. It's an expression of ideas, concerns, values and desires and it's very personal to the person making the comment, and to the intended recipients. When we understand that social media has a high degree of personal emotional impetus we get a steer in how to respond appropriately.

It's essential that you start by allowing your customers to use social media as a specific channel of communication with your company. Create accounts with Facebook and Twitter specifically with the function of encouraging comment from the general public. Many businesses already do this highly successfully, I follow Tesco, which has set up a Twitter account specifically for customers to communicate problems and it works incredibly well! Monitor your accounts constantly throughout the day and arrange your settings to notify you of any 'mentions'. This way you're going to be on top of any negative comments pretty quickly and this is essential.

Businesses are fearful of social media because they're frightened of the impact on their business reputation of negative comments from the general public. In fact I have known businesses that do whatever they can to avoid getting any feedback, just in case it's something they really don't want to hear and they do this by steering away from it wherever possible. This reaction is not untypical and can only be described as an ostrich with its head in the sand.

If this is you or perhaps you think you don't do enough to evaluate what your customers think, you need to change NOW!

I'm afraid that the advent of feedback though social media is something you cannot avoid and you ignore at your peril. Let me give you some stats, current at the time of writing:

- The average Twitter user has 126 followers (source: Guardian)
- The average Facebook user has 130 friends (source: Facebook)

It's not uncommon for social media savvy people to use both media and link them together and it's important to note that facebook friends are not necessarily the same people that would follow you on twitter. The impact then of any one negative comment about a business or service could have an immediate impact on as many as 256 individuals. This means that for every dozen individuals posting negative comment on your business more than 3,000 people hear about it! It's simply not possible (or commercial) to ignore this.

Yet social media goes beyond just comment from customers, it also is increasingly used to evaluate businesses, products and services before purchase. In fact there are already many specialist rating sites that allow you to read customer comments before deciding where to buy and I don't believe it will be long before online search engine providers start using customer ratings as part of their search criteria. That will mean that businesses providing poor customer service will not be featuring well on the search engine rankings no matter what they spend on optimisation.

There is nothing to fear here.

As I have said all along any feedback we receive is an opportunity for us to shine and, even negative feedback shared on a common platform for all to see should be viewed as a public stage on which to perform our excellent customer service skills.

It's easy to go wrong here if you forget the basics explained in this book. I watch (sometimes in dismay) businesses that think that the correct response to negative feedback through social media or rating sites is to flood the media with fictitious glowing accounts from friends, staff and colleagues of made up visits or purchases.

This achieves nothing, let's not forget that customers are not stupid. They will see right through this and if you are ever discovered deliberately falsifying customer experiences the PR impact will very likely be terminal.

The correct response requires you to acknowledge the customer's concerns, take ownership and address the points raised (as described in some detail earlier in this book). Social media gives you a platform against which you can show a disgruntled customer (and everybody they're connected to) that their concerns are important to you and that you value them as a customer.

When you consider that when you're responding to an individual comment or complaint that you are addressing many more people than just the one correspondent it won't take you long to work out that this is a perfect advertising/marketing/PR opportunity. If you respond quickly, address the concerns and go the extra mile to really show that you value the customer, you will create a WOW moment that will be shared by hundreds. This is the true value of social media, knowing that you've got a problem and turning this into a positive sales message.

All of this is relatively straight forward and if you want to get an idea just how much your customers comments have permeated social media just do a Google search on your company name along with say "comments", "customer service" or "feedback". This will give you a really good idea of just what potential customers are finding out about your company before they decide to buy. And if you find anything that's not good, deal with it there and then!

To summarise, social media is just another communication channel that you need to tap into. If you have a clear customer focus and apply the things you have learnt in this book the rest should just be plain sailing.

Distress purchases – acquisition by necessity not desire

There are certain things in life we buy because we have to, not because we want to. These things are given the dubious title of a 'distress purchase' and include the likes of insurance, repair services, perhaps a washing machine and so on.

It's incredibly hard to create a great customer experience from the environment of a distress purchase – it's quite likely that your customer wants the whole process done as quickly and cheaply as possible. How can you build advocacy in this environment? It's a tough one, but interestingly enough most of the principals described in this book still apply.

For starters we need to emphasise with our customer, we need to recognise that this would not necessarily be a purchase of choice. We then need to think about the customer's expectation level when it comes to making this purchase and where we have the opportunity to exceed this expectation. We need to be attentive and do what we can to show the customer that we want and would appreciate their custom.

I would like to say that some customers make distressed purchases purely on cost – and that I would know because I'm one of them. I can't think of any time that I have ever purchased my car insurance based on the service I received during the purchase. Then again maybe that's because nobody wowed me enough to think differently.

I believe that customers making distress purchases are no less subject to the content of this book as any other. It's true that the purchase is enforced rather than desired, but that doesn't mean that the customer would not be impressed with an organisation that understood their requirements, exceeded their expectations and showed that they valued their business.

Is it a more complex relationship? I guess so, marginally. You may have to give it some more thought and the answers may not be so obvious, but nonetheless you can still achieve positive advocacy if you work hard at it.

Seven things to make your customer service stand out

I hope that you have found the material in this book challenging and useful and that you have changed the way you think about your relationships with your customers. In this section I want to provide you with a summary of seven key things you need to do to make your customer service stand out from your competitors.

Most of these are covered in detail within the pages of this book, so you can refer back as you need to – this is a quick fire list that you can use every day to remind you of your objectives.

Many of my clients take these points and convert them into a set of benchmarks, a frame work of rules to guide their staff and ensure that everyone knows the standards to which they aspire. The key is to come back to this section time and time again to remind yourself of the key changes you need to make in your business and to check your progress.

Some of these you will get relatively quickly, others will be much harder to achieve. However any and all progress you achieve will make a difference to your business and differentiate you from your competitors.

Never rest on your laurels.

These changes cannot be a set of targets to be reached, I think it unlikely that you can ever say "we always do that". Customer service involves people and changing mindsets will be a constant challenge. These points are more a gauge to measure yourself against, objectives to be worked towards, reviewed and constantly evaluated. You should share them with your staff, give them all a copy so that everyone is clear as to what you expect of them. Above all, don't get complacent – it's when you really think you have it pegged that your standards will drop and you will slip backwards.

Customer service and experience isn't a one off job to be ticked off the list, it's a constant within your business that needs continuous attention, refinement and focus.

1.   Always put the customer first.

I can't stress to your enough how important this.

It's not by accident that I have put this at number one and at the top of my list. It is the single most important thing you can do to create a customer focused business that delivers a great customer experience.

Make no mistake, this will be a challenge. The premise is relatively easy to understand but putting it into practice is a whole new ball game.

Let me summarise it for you as I have for many of my clients in this one hard and fast rule that should NEVER be broken:

There is no process, action or function that you do will ever take precedent over serving the customer.

Be absolutely clear here in terms of what this means — I think it's pretty straightforward but even some of my very best clients struggle to make this clear to their staff.

This goes back mainly to process driven staff that find it hard to stop what they're doing to serve a customer. They see it as acceptable to perhaps finish laying the table or stacking the shelf, before turning their attention to the customer.

It's not.

Worse still, there will be staff in your organisation that will think this doesn't apply to them. Perhaps because they work in accounts or behind the scenes and not in a customer facing role. Let me be specific — this rule applies to absolutely everyone in your business regardless of position or function.

2.   Ask them what they think.

Here's a quote for you from Ross Perot, American business tycoon and Presidential Candidate: "You would be surprised how many companies don't listen to their customers."

In simple terms if you want your business to survive, prosper and grow then you need to give your customers more of what they like and less of what they don't like — the only way you can be certain to know this is to ask them.

We have looked at how to engage customers in feedback extensively in this book — look back to remind yourself. Remember a good feedback exercise is one that lets the customer say what they want.

I promise you — feedback will be an incredibly useful tool for you to look after your customers and get a great steer on how to take your business forward.

3.   Recognise and resolve issues right away!

When your customers take the time to make you aware of issues they're giving you the opportunity to put it right. Reacting quickly and professionally supports your customer's decision to buy from your company and can create overwhelming advocacy. Stronger affinities are created when the customer knows from personal experience that you really do care and are prepared to demonstrate this.

This is the positive loop of affirmation that takes disillusioned purchasers and turns them into customers for life. Make sure you and your team get the skills you need to deal with unhappy customers, knowing how to care for a customer is a skill in itself — and one that needs to be learned.

One final thing — never abdicate responsibility for responding to a customer's concerns to one of your staff. It will give your customers the impression that they're not important to you and will highlight your ineffectiveness as a manager.

4.   Build relationships by remembering your customers

Nobody wants to feel dispensable, just a number, one of a million other customers. We all want to be appreciated and treated as an individual. Put processes in place wherever you can to treat each customer as if they were your only customer.

Recording or remembering customers' personal details like their names, what they buy, specific circumstances like perhaps if they work night shifts and don't like early morning calls, or previous concerns they may have raised — all are key. It shows effort on your part to create a more personable environment that is welcoming and engaging, making a visit to your premises a pleasurable one.

Carry this through every communication you have with your customers and you will develop a personal engagement that competitors will find hard, if not impossible to break.

It's not essential to know names, many of you working in retail environments may not be able to capture or record previous purchases – but you will know which of your customers are regulars - you will probably recognise their faces. Make sure you show this to your customers, sometimes it can be as simple as "hello again" – an easy way to show you recognise their continuing patronage.

5.   Make sure you show your customers that you value their business

Just because your customers buy from you regularly doesn't mean they always will. Start by asking yourself: "What value am I giving my customers this time around?"

If you want to increase repeat business start by giving something away! Don't be frightened by this, it's an initiative used by major businesses to drive repeat purchases, but make sure you do it properly. Giving your customers additional services, goods or discounts has much more impact if it has an intrinsic value to them. Clever and targeted offers require less expenditure for greater impact value, so make sure that your offers are relevant.

Doing this well shows your customers that you are interested enough in them to recognise and offer discounts on goods and services that they actually buy. It also shows that you value their business, knowing as they do that you need not provide such offers on things that they are likely to buy in any case.

This is a tried and tested method that secures long-term repeat business and generates significant brand loyalty.

6.   Promise good – deliver great!

Always leave yourself a reasonable margin when making promises to deliver services or goods. This way if things don't go as planned you have allowed a tolerance which should mean you won't disappoint the customer.
    Better still, if things do go as planned you will be able to delight your customers with and earlier than expected pleasant surprise. This supports the purchase experience generating great positive advocacy.

Simple!

7.   Be on the front foot – manage your customers expectations.

Don't wait for your customer to chase you – be on the front foot and contact them first!

- If a customer ever has to chase you - you've failed!
- If you're ever late – you've failed!
- If the customer turns up and you're not ready – you've failed!
- If it's not what the customer expected – you've failed!

This is all about communicating pro-actively with your customers and not waiting for them to contact you. It's about keeping them in the picture so that they know what to expect at every step of the way. For example, there's never any need to be late – being late is when you arrive at a time after you're expected. Call ahead and let the customer know you are running behind and when you arrive at a later time, it will be as expected.

If you take a pro-active approach when communicating with your customers you're showing them that you really value their business and this is fundamental in building the advocacy you need to create a customer for life.

Close

Our world is changing.

Customers are becoming more demanding and their expectations are higher than ever. Increased competition makes it harder than ever to compete on price alone and so successful businesses recognise the need to establish a great customer experience.

I hope that you have found the content of this book useful. I have no doubt that you will find some of it challenging, but whoever said great customer service would be easy?

I want to leave you with one of my favourite ever phrases, that to me summarises everything I have detailed in this book. It's so simple yet evokes the essence of your approach.

"If you don't look after your customers, somebody else will!"